GUSTAV STICKLEY: ORIGINATOR OF CRAFTSMAN HOUSES AND CRAFTS-
MAN FURNITURE: FOUNDER AND EDITOR OF THE CRAFTSMAN MAGAZINE.

MORE CRAFTSMAN HOMES

Floor Plans and Illustrations for
78 Mission Style Dwellings

by

GUSTAV STICKLEY

Dover Publications, Inc., New York

The Craftsman idea makes for the development in this country of an art and architecture which shall express the spirit of the American people; for the creation of conditions which shall provide the best home environment for our children; for a form of industrial education which shall enable men and women to earn their own living.

Published in Canada by General Publishing Company, Ltd., 30 Lesmill Road, Don Mills, Toronto, Ontario.

Published in the United Kingdom by Constable and Company, Ltd.

This Dover edition, first published in 1982, is an unabridged republication of the work originally published by The Craftsman Publishing Company, New York, in 1912 under the title *More Craftsman Homes.*

International Standard Book Number: 0-486-24252-8

Manufactured in the United States of America
Dover Publications, Inc.
180 Varick Street
New York, N.Y. 10014

Library of Congress Cataloging in Publication Data

Stickley, Gustav, 1858-1942.
　More Craftsman homes.

　Reprint. Originally published: New York : Craftsman Publishing, 1912.
　1. Architecture, Domestic—Mission style—Designs and plans. 2. Architecture, Modern—20th century—United States—Designs and plans. I. Title.
NA7208.S75　1982　　　728.3'7'0223　　　81-17403
ISBN 0-486-24252-8 (pbk.)　　　　　　　　AACR2

TABLE OF CONTENTS

	PAGE
A Word About Craftsman Architecture: By Gustav Stickley	1
The Relation of Craftsman Architecture to Country Living	5
The House of the Democrat: By William L. Price	7
Practical Craftsman Cement House Planned for Beauty and Convenience	11
Cement House Showing Interesting Roof Treatment and Roomy Homelike Interior	14
Three-Story Craftsman Bungalow Suitable for a Hillside Site	16
Craftsman Cement Dwelling Inspired by Old-Fashioned New England Farmhouse	19
Simple Cement Cottage for a Small Family	22
Inexpensive One-Story Bungalow with Effective Use of Trellis	24
Small One-Story Cement Bungalow with Slate Roof, Designed for a Narrow Lot	26
Cement House with Pergola, Sleeping Balcony and Practical Interesting Interior	28
Plaster Dwelling for Town or Country	30
Commodious Cement House with Terrace, Porches and Sleeping Balconies	32
Cement House, Compact yet Spacious, Suitable for a City Street	34
Large Cement House for Town or Country	36
Concrete or Plaster House of Moderate Size and Simple Design	38
Inexpensive Cement and Shingle Cottage	40
Craftsman House Designed for a Narrow Lot	42
Small Two-Story Cement House with Recessed Porch and Balcony	44
Craftsman Cement House, Simple, Comfortable and Spacious	46
Small but Roomy One-Story Cement Bungalow Planned for Simplified Housekeeping	49
Concrete Cottage with Comfortable Interior, Designed to Admit Ample Light	51
Inexpensive Cement Construction for Summer and Week-End One-Story Bungalow	53
Two-Story Cement Bungalow with Ample Porch Room and Comfortable Interior	54
Two-Story House for Village Corner Plot	56
Moderate-Sized Craftsman House Combining Both Privacy and Hospitality	58
Craftsman House Designed for City or Suburban Lot	60
Cement Cottage for a Narrow Town Lot	62
Inexpensive and Homelike Cottage of Stone and Shingle, for Simple Housekeeping	64
Stone and Shingle House with Seven Rooms and Recessed Entrance Porch	66
Roomy Craftsman House in which Stone, Cement and Wood Are Used	68
Craftsman Stone House with Practical Built-in Fittings	70
Rough Stone House Combining Comfort and Picturesqueness	72
Eight-Room Bungalow of Stone and Cement	75
Craftsman Cottage of Stone, Shingle and Slate: A Practical and Comfortable Home	77
Brick Cottage with Convenient Built-in Furnishings and Ample Porch Room	79
Two-Story House of Stone, Brick and Cement, with Typical Craftsman Interior	81
Craftsman House of Tapestry Brick with Porches, Balcony and Spacious Interior	85
Brick House with Many Homelike Features	88
City House with Interesting Façade and Sleeping Balcony and Homelike Interior	90
Craftsman City House with Second-Story Porch and Third-Story Sleeping Balcony	92
Inexpensive Cottage for a Small Family	95

TABLE OF CONTENTS

PAGE

Moderate-Sized Brick House, with Recessed Porch and Pleasant, Homelike Rooms . . 97
Rural One-Story Bungalow of Field Stone 99
One-Story Craftsman Bungalow Planned on Simple and Economic Lines 100
Two-Story Country Bungalow Made Comfortable with Much Built-in Furniture . . . 102
Shingled House with Spacious Living Room and Sheltered Porches 105
Comfortable Shingled House with Built-in Fittings and Sleeping Porches 107
Shingled House with Ample Provision for Outdoor Living 109
Shingled Cottage Suitable for Country, Seaside or Suburban Life 111
Practical Six-Room Shingled Cottage 113
Small Craftsman Farmhouse of Stone and Shingles, Simple and Homelike in Design . . 114
Craftsman Rural Dwelling Combining Beauty, Comfort and Convenience 116
Farmhouse Designed for Utility and Comfort 118
Comfortable, Convenient, Homelike Farmhouse with Connected Woodshed and Barn . 120
Compactly Built Craftsman Farmhouse 122
Practical, Inexpensive One-Story Bungalow 124
Seven-Room Shingled Craftsman Cottage 126
Shingled Cottage with Recessed Porches 128
Small Shingled House with Right Use of Structural Features and Woodwork 130
Rustic Bungalow with Open Upper Story 132
Summer Bungalow with Open Attic 134
Rustic One-Story Bungalow, with Compact Interior and Comfortable Fittings 135
One-Story Shingled Craftsman Bungalow for Rural Surroundings 137
Ten-Room House for Town or Country Life 138
Compact Two-Story Craftsman House Planned for Sloping Site 140
Craftsman Farmhouse Planned for Comfortable Home Life 142
Typical One-Story Craftsman Bungalow Suitable for Either Summer or All-Year Use . 144
Architectural Development of the Log Cabin in America 146
The Log House Built at Craftsman Farms 147
Log Cottage for Summer Camp or Permanent Country Home 152
Small but Comfortable Log Dwelling 154
Little Wood Cottage Arranged for Simple Country Living 156
Comfortable One-Story Bungalow of Logs 158
Permanent Summer Camp of Logs with Top Story Arranged for Outdoor Sleeping . . 160
Log Bungalow for Summer Use with Covered Porch and Partially Open Sleeping Room 162
Craftsman Country Schoolhouse of Logs 164
Rural Shingled Schoolhouse Planned with Connecting Workroom 166
Craftsman Gardens for Craftsman Homes 168
Pergolas in American Gardens 177
Two Brick Bungalows with Cypress Gables 183
Concrete Bungalows: Economy of Construction Attained by the Way the Forms Are Used 189
The Craftsman Fireplace: A Complete Heating and Ventilating System 198

A WORD ABOUT CRAFTSMAN ARCHITECTURE

ROM the beginning of my work as a craftsman my object has been to develop types of houses and house furnishings that are essentially cheerful, durable and appropriate for the kind of life I believe the intelligent American public desires. It comes to me every day of my life that a home spirit is being awakened amongst us, that as a nation we are beginning to realize how important it is to have homes of our own, homes that we like, that we have been instrumental in building, that we will want to have belong to our children. And, of course, this means that the homes must be honest and beautiful dwellings; they must be built to last; they must be so well planned that we want them to last, and yet they must be within our means. The delusion that a really beautiful home is within the reach of only the very rich is losing ground, as is its sister delusion that only by the slavish imitation of foreign models is æsthetic satisfaction to be achieved. People are also awakening to the fact that beauty in a building is not merely a matter of decoration, a something to be added at will, but is inherent in the lines and masses of the structure itself.

The point of view of the New England farmer, whose instructions to the architect were: "I'll build my house, and you fetch along your architecture and nail it on," is no longer typical. Today if you find a farmer who is thinking about building a home, the chances are that he and his family and the town builder spend a lot of evenings around the farm dining table, poring over plans and blue prints, and probably sketches which the farmer himself has made. There is no suggestion about an Italian villa or a French chateau, but the farmer is probably saying, "We want a large room to live in; we want an open fire in it because it looks cheerful and the children like it; we want a kitchen that my wife won't mind working in, and we want the house light and warm and pretty." This is a great change from the old days, and is in line with the theory on which Craftsman architecture is founded,—namely, a style of building suited to the lives of the people, having the best possible structural outline, the simplest form, materials that belong to the country in which the house is built and colors that please and cheer.

The Craftsman type of building is largely the result not of elaboration, but of elimination. The more I design, the more sure I am that elimination is the secret of beauty in architecture. By this I do not mean that I want to think scantily and work meagerly. Rather, I feel that one should plan richly and fully, and then begin to prune, to weed, to shear away everything that seems superfluous and superficial. Practically every house I build I find, both in structural outline and in the planning and the adjustment of the interior space, that I am simplifying, that I am doing away with something that was not needed; that I am using my spaces to better advantage. All of this means the expenditure of less money and the gain of more comfort and beauty.

It is only when we to an extent begin at the beginning of these things that we come to know how much that is superfluous we have added to life, and how fearful we have been to be straightforward and honest in any artistic expression. Why may we not build just the house we want, so that it belongs to our lives and expresses them? I have, all too slowly, begun to realize that it is right to build houses as people wish them, to cut away ornament, to subordinate tradition, and to put into the structure and into the interior finish the features that the occupants will find comfortable and convenient, and which almost inevitably result in beauty for them. It seems to me that every man should have the right to think out the plan for his house to suit himself, and then the architect should make this plan into a reasonable structure; that is, the outline should be well-proportioned and the different parts should be brought together so that the structural perfection will result in decorative beauty. If, added to this simple reasonable structure, the materials for the house are so far as possible those which may be found in the locality where the house is built, a beauty of fitness is gained at the very start. A house that is built of stone where stones are in the fields, of concrete where the soil is sandy, of brick where brick can be had reasonably, or of wood if the house is in a mountainous wooded region, will from the beginning belong to the landscape. And the result is not only harmony but economy. Why should the man who lives on a hillside bring brick from a long distance when the most interesting of modern dwellings, the log house, is at his hand? Or, if the brick could be had from the kiln a few miles away, why seek logs which are made expensive by the long freight haul from far-away mountains, and which would not seem in any way harmonious with the country where trees are scarce?

Once having settled upon the style of house which must suit the lie of the land and the happiness of the owner, the arrangement of floor spaces is next in significance. First of all, do away with any sense of elaboration and with the idea that a house must be a series of cells, room upon room, shut away from all others. Have a living room, the "great room" of the house that corresponds to the old "great hall" of ancient dwellings. This space is the opportunity for people to come together, to sit around the fireplace, for there must always be an open fire. It is the room where people read or study or work evenings, or play or dance, as the case may be,—the place where the elderly members of the family will have the greatest comfort and contentment, and where the children will store up memories that can never die. This great room must be well lighted, it will have groups of windows that furnish cheerful vistas in the daytime, and it must be so planned that seats or divans circle the fireplace and bring, by the very structure of the house, the family into intimate, happy relationship. It is wise, of course, that the entrance to this room from out of doors should be through an entry way or vestibule, in order that drafts may not be felt and to furnish coat room and opportunities for the putting aside of heavy wraps, umbrellas, etc. This should be borne in mind especially in cold climates where the whole comfort of the room may be sacrificed to a too abrupt connection with out of doors.

In the planning of this first floor and the adjustment of the spaces I have as few entrances and doorways as possible. They are expensive; they use up space, prevent a look of coziness and lessen the opportunities for building in of interesting fittings. It is also economical and picturesque to group the windows, and always the built-in fittings, the bookcases, the corner seats should be adjusted to the light from the windows as well as the fireplace. But here, as in the outside structure, I find the process of elimination must be always borne in mind. I do away with everything that does not contribute to comfort and beauty. This is a safe rule. The charm of the living room can be greatly enhanced by the alcove dining room, a greater sense of space is added and all the things that are put in the dining room to make it beautiful contribute to the pleasure of the people who are sitting in the living room. Also, the pleasure in the dining room is enhanced by glimpses of the living room, its spaces, its open fires, its grouped windows. This does away also with one partition; it furnishes opportunity for the interesting use of screens, or for the half-partition, on top of which may be placed lines of books or jars of ferns, not expensive ornaments for the house, and adding greatly to the beauty of color and to the homelike quality.

The question of built-in fittings is one that I feel is an essential part of the Craftsman idea in architecture. I have felt from the beginning of my work that a house should be live-in-able when it is finished. Why should one enter one's dwelling and find that it is a barren uninviting prisonlike spot, until it is loaded with furniture and the walls hidden under pictures and picture frames? I contend that when the builder leaves the house, it should be a place of good cheer, a place that holds its own welcome forever. This, of course, can only be accomplished by the building in of furnishings that are essentially structural features, and by the planning of the finishing of the walls and the woodwork so that they are a part of the inherent beauty of the home, and not mere backgrounds for endless unrelated decorations. In my own houses I study the color of the interior when I am designing the house. I plan the woodwork so that it embraces the built-in fittings, so that every bookcase or corner seat is a part of the development of the woodwork. In no other way can a house be made beautiful, or the architecture of the interior be complete and homelike.

You cannot make your house and your furnishings two separate schemes of attractiveness and expect an harmonious whole. The reason that this has been so much done in America is because people have not owned their homes. Usually their furniture alone belongs to them, and *that* they have tried to select so that it would be pleasant and well related. They have adjusted it to the houses that they have chanced to live in as well as they could, until they have grown to feel that a house is one thing and furnishings quite another. This is especially true in city apartments, where people expect to remain only a few years before they move on to another set of inconveniences. The furniture which in one house was adjusted to mahogany and green walls is later on adjusted to yellow oak and pink walls. And so families have gone from one set of torturing surroundings to another, until it seems a miracle that any sense of color and proportion in house furnishings should survive.

As for my own houses, I realize that they more or less demand the sort of furniture that I have been in the habit of planning for them. Not because I hold to one narrow outlook of beauty, but because I cannot but see that most of the imitation antiques as well as the types of modern furniture made purely for department store sales are not adjusted to simple practical artistic home surroundings. In the planning of my houses I have so eliminated the superfluous in structure, in floor plans, in interior fittings, that furniture which is not well planned or is overornamented must of necessity seem out of place.

"More Craftsman Homes," which is the second book of houses that I have published, stands for my own ideal of house building. In other words, it shows the extent to which I have been able in my own, perhaps small, way, to achieve

A WORD ABOUT CRAFTSMAN ARCHITECTURE

beauty in architecture through this process of elimination. It makes clear how I feel about houses which are built on economical principles, on good structural lines, always with the ideal of beauty, always insisting upon the utmost comfort and convenience. The edition (20,000) of the first book, "Craftsman Homes," which was published over two years ago, is now exhausted. And so great has been the demand for a book of Craftsman houses that we have found it necessary, in order to meet the response of the people who are interested in this kind of architecture, to get out within the last few months the book to which this little talk forms the introduction. This book in some respects is scarcely more than a catalogue. It is merely a straightforward presentation of my more recent designs in Craftsman houses suited for building in concrete, in stone, in brick and in wood. Many of these houses have already been built and have been found most satisfactory by their owners. Several of them have been built on Craftsman Farms, my own home place in New Jersey. I feel that every time a Craftsman house is built I verify in my own mind my ideal of architecture; that is, beauty through elimination.

There can be no doubt in my mind that a native type of architecture is growing up in America. I am not prepared to say to what extent the Craftsman idea has contributed to it, but I do know, from a very wide correspondence, that people all over the country are asking for houses in which they may be comfortable, houses which will be appropriate backgrounds for their own lives and right starting points for the lives of their children. It is my own wish, my own final ideal, that the Craftsman house may so far as possible meet this demand and be instrumental in helping to establish in America a higher ideal, not only of beautiful architecture, but of home life.

THE RELATION OF CRAFTSMAN ARCHITECTURE TO COUNTRY LIVING

IN THE development of Craftsman architecture I have had in mind especially the need of better dwellings for suburbs and country, and although I have also designed houses for city and town, most of the plans are intended for a rural environment. I believe that on the right use of the land depends much of our national welfare, and that therefore farm life should be made not only effective and profitable but also pleasant. I realize that the normal existence is one which includes an all-round development of the faculties, a wholesome proportion of manual and mental labor, opportunities for spiritual growth; and so I believe that a form of building which makes for simplicity of housekeeping and provides ample chance for outdoor working and living will help to increase the health, happiness and efficiency of the people.

My effort, therefore, has been directed toward something that will make country life more interesting. I see no reason why people should not build comfortable houses in the country, and make for themselves the kind of surroundings that will prove an incentive and inspiration, instead of the ugly buildings, tawdry furnishings and the many inconveniences which now make farm life so unattractive. Why should the advantages of our civilization be confined to the cities and towns? If they are to be of real value to the people at large, is it not imperative that they should be shared by the guardians of those natural resources from which the city draws its strength? And is it not an inadequate and one-sided sort of progress which gives to one set of workers those comforts and conveniences which modern science has devised, and leaves the others in conditions of discomfort and drudgery?

This lack of balance, I believe, can be adjusted to a great extent by the right kind of rural architecture. In the case of the farm, not only is it possible to plan the buildings and arrange the work on a basis of economy and convenience, but it is also possible to make the interior of the house so attractive that the housewife as well as the farmer will find it a place of daily pleasure and contentment. But it is essential for this that we simplify most of our present complicated ideals of cooking, ornament, apparel and furnishing; that we construct more convenient and comfortable homes; that we employ labor-saving devices for the house as well as for the barns and the fields. Especially is this needed for the woman who now turns in disgust from the overwork and isolation of the country to the city with its artificial amusements. By the use of labor-saving devices, by more scientific methods of housekeeping, by the simplifying of ways of living and thinking, what is now a heartbreaking drudgery can be made a source of joy and pride.

The house can be so planned that it will be a factor in the growth and happiness of the people. The large living room with its central fireplace will form the nucleus of home life, a place for rest and entertainment, for the gathering of the family and the planning of whatever industries are being developed on the farm. The piazza at the back will serve to connect house and garden and encourage outdoor living, and a dining porch will permit the joy of meals served in the open. The provision of a summer kitchen will bring fresh air and brightness to many tasks that would be wearisome indoors. The laundry tubs may be placed here instead of down cellar, thus saving time and steps and making labor less irksome. Here also can be done the cooking, preserving and canning of fruits and vegetables, the cleaning of milk cans, the preparing of food for the stock. In short, both house and housework can be so adjusted as to make labor a pleasure and the country home a center of interest.

And with the bettering of conditions in home and farm a new spirit will enter into our tasks. We shall readjust our attitude toward work. Instead of submitting to it as one of life's necessary evils, we shall welcome it with courage and with joy, as the thing through which we get our greatest development.

Not only does such a type of architecture as that which we advocate form an incentive and inspiration to country living, but it tends to promote a coöperative spirit. People are willing to coöperate if they can get more comfort into their lives, and keep better in touch with progress. And in the necessary development of rural life, problems of lighting, water supply, sewerage, farm machinery, motive power, etc., as well as of social and educational needs, will have to be solved by coöperation. Then with the increase of common material interests there will come a strengthening of spiritual ties. In place of the old feeling of rural isolation we shall find a quickening of the recreative and intellectual life of the people. Community spirit and community pride will become factors in the betterment of rural conditions, until every dweller of township, village, farm and open country will enjoy a share in the responsibilities and privileges of happy community life, and so contribute to the progress of the nation.

It was with this point of view that I started to organize Craftsman Farms, to demonstrate what could be done to bring interest, efficiency and beauty into country living. While we have a number of buildings there already, we expect later on to have a good many more, and from time to time we shall publish in THE CRAFTSMAN pictures, plans and descriptions of the houses, stables and shops we may build. The illustrations and plans of the Log House which we are showing on page 147 will give some idea of what we have accomplished in this direction, and the latch string is always out for anyone who is planning to build or who cares to see what we are doing.

G. S.

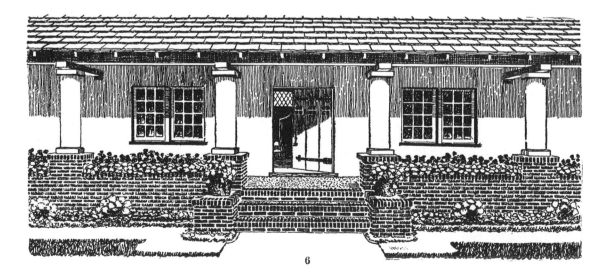

THE HOUSE OF THE DEMOCRAT: BY WILLIAM L. PRICE

"And what wealth then shall be left us when
    none shall gather gold,
To buy his friend in the market, and pinch and
    pine the sold?

"Nay, what save the lovely city, and the little
    house on the hill,
And the wastes and the woodland beauty and
    the happy fields we till."

Y DEFINITION of Democracy is a state wherein there is no special privilege; my definition of a democrat is one who of his own impulse can truly say with Walt Whitman, "By God, I will not have anything that every man may not have the counterpart of on like terms." Not the "Thou shalt not" of extraneous force, but the "I will not" of self-control and brotherliness. And the House of the Democrat? It must need no special privilege for its gaining, and it must not oppress by its possession.

I once built a house for a Democrat,—a man who left a money-making partnership when he believed he had as much money as he could employ profitably to his fellowmen,—and his one concern for this house was not that it should cost too much, but that it should in no wise embarrass his friends: ample enough to contain them; simple enough to leave them unoppressed; yet with artistry to please and to lead them, if they would, to do likewise. Some of his friends were not well enough off to afford such a house, some of them were rich enough to build palaces; yet his house was not to make the one envious or the other contemptuous.

But such a house is only possible to the real Democrat, the man who demands equality of opportunity without desiring an *impossible* equality of attainment. A man may, perhaps I should say, must be a stately gentleman to be such a Democrat. His possessions may be many or few and his house great or small, but to have arrived at the dignity of democracy is to have arrived at stateliness. To have in your possession nothing that is not by right your own, to ask no favor but comradeship, to demand no rights but equal rights, to produce and get the equivalent, to be able to give of yourself rather than of your goods, —this were an achievement that would gild a cottage, or make simply human the stateliest habitation.

But no man can be a Democrat by himself, however many sturdy steps he may take toward it or however his heart may swell with the hope of it. "We be of one flesh, you and I," and we neither live to ourselves nor build to ourselves nor by ourselves. A man may by a wish set the feet of the whole world toward democracy, but the house of the democrat can only be built by the willing hands of democrats, so as there are few democratic architects and few democratic craftsmen there are few democratic houses.

Look at your own houses, my friends, the houses of your friends, and the houses that line your roadways. You may find, here and there, an old farmhouse springing out of the soil, built by village carpenter and mason and smith, with low roofs and wide-spreading porches that mothers its human brood as the hen its tired chicks,—and when you find it, your heart will yearn to it; you will feel that a Jefferson might have spoken his noblest thoughts under its rooftree and the simplest yeoman his simplest hopes for tomorrow's crops with an equal dignity and an even fitness.

THE HOUSE OF THE DEMOCRAT

I do not mean the pillared porticoes of the stately mansions of Colonial days; they speak of pomp, of powdered wig, of brocade gown, of small clothes and small sword, of coach and four, of slavery or serfdom; nor do I speak of the lesser imitations of such houses. When Jefferson and Washington spoke of democracy, they spoke not of what was, but of what *was to be;* they spoke of democrats in spite of kings, of democracy in spite of palaces.

AND we who have built up privileges and powers and potentates in the the name of democracy, we who have reëstablished the power of dead men and their deeds over the living, we who have repudiated Jefferson's "The earth belongs in usufruct to the living," we who in this civilization of stupid waste play shuttlecock to the barbaric battledores of roaring Hells and stifling pens,—what should we know of the house of the democrat? We are fastening tighter the rule of the past in the name of education and taste; we are forging chains of "wisdom" and knowledge and riveting them on the arms of Prophecy; setting up styles in art at the mandates of established orders of taste, just as our "Supreme Courts" are binding the hands of Tomorrow with the precedents of yesterday, as if there were any supreme court but the people whose hands they vainly try to bind, or any canon of taste more holy than fitness. Our laws are like our houses, cluttered up with imitations of the outworn junk of other days.

There is scarcely a molding in your house that is not stupidly copied or perverted from some lost meaning expressed by men of other days in the building of temple or palace; no stupid, dirty, wooden baluster that had not its inception in crook-kneed debasement to an unhallowed state, no ornament that does not reek of the pride of place and power; shield and wreath, festoon and torch, they speak no word to us at all, and if they could speak would tell only of the pomps and prides of other days, of an order that has passed in the flesh even in those old lands where the people still hang the remnants and insignia of powers gone on their sham princes and powerless potentates, and even the spirit of that false pride is dead, for they produce no new emblems, no new visible manifestations of rank and power, but are content to paw over the tawdry finery of the past.

And, however, with our lips we have repudiated those shams—in our spirits we still kiss the feet of place and pomp; we still glorify hereditary power; we still hold up its hands to our own undoing, and we still copy so far as we can its vainglorious essays at expression. Our dress at a few cents the yard must ape their gorgeousness, our models must come from Paris even if our goods come from Kensington, and are made up in loathsome sweat-shops. Our furnishings, tossed out by machines and held together by the grace of imitation varnish, and our houses tacked together, putty-filled, mean in workmanship and mean in design, lick the feet of a pompous past, bow down in worship of a time that, at least, had the conviction of its sins, and openly elected to be lorded over by privileged classes.

WHEN at last we build the house of the democrat, its doors shall be wide and unbarred, for why should men steal who are free to make? It shall be set in a place of greenery, for the world is a large place and its loveliness mostly a wilderness; it shall be far enough away from its next for privacy and not too far for neighborliness; it shall have a little space knit within a garden wall; flowers shall creep up to its warmth, and flow, guided, but unrebuked, over wall and low-drooped eaves. It shall neither be built in poverty and haste, nor abandoned in prosperity; it shall grow as the family grows; it shall have rooms enough for the privacy of each and the fellowship of all. Its arms shall spread wide enough to gather in a little measure of the common earth, for your democracy will provide leisure and your democrat will not only pluck flowers but will grow them, not only eat the fruits of the earth but will find joy in planting, in "seed time and harvest," and all the myriad days of growth between will look to the sundial rather than the timetable for the ordering of his day.

The rooms of his house shall be ample, and low, wide-windowed, deep-seated, spacious, cool by reason of shadows in summer, warm by the ruddy glow of firesides in winter, open to wistful summer airs, tight closed against the wintry blasts: a house, a home, a shrine; a little democracy unjealous of the greater world, and pouring forth the spirit of its own sure justness for the commonwealth.

Its walls shall be the quiet background for the loveliness of life, hung over with the few records of our own and others' growth made in the playtime of art; its furnishings the product of that art's more serious hours; its implements from kitchen-ware to dressing table touched by the sane and hallowing hand of purpose and taste.

This is the house of the Democrat, and of such houses shall the democracy be full: none so humble that it may not touch the hem of art; none so great that the hand of art, whose other name is service, shall have passed it by.

When the tale of our hours of labor is a tale of hours of joy; when the workshop has ceased to be a gloomy hell from which we drag our debased bodies for a few hours of gasping rest; when the workshop shall rather be a temple where we joyously bring our best to lay it on the shrine of service; when art shall mean work and work shall mean art to the humblest,—then democracy shall be real; then shall our hours be too short for the joy of living; then patiently shall we build up a civilization that shall endure; then shall we laugh at the slips of our eagerness, and no more remember the horrid gorgon-headed monster, privilege, whose merest glance turned the hearts of men to stone, set nation against nation, armed man's heels to crush his fellows, fenced our coast from our fellow men, built strong portaled prisons, armed ships to kill, filled our hearts with devastating fear, clouded our clear sight and spilled the lives and hopes of the many, and stole their hard-bought wealth for the bedecking of her snaky tresses— then shall we build the house of the Democrat.

And when the Democrat has built his house, when free men have housed themselves to meet their present need and have no fear that the need of tomorrow shall cry at their doors unmet,—then shall men and women and little children, out of the fulness of their lives, out of the free gift of their surplus hours, build for each and for all, such parks and pleasure places, such palaces of the people, such playhouses, such temples, as men have not yet known. And the men and women and children shall find playtime to use them; find time and powers out of their work to write plays and play them, to write poems and sing them, to carve, to paint, to teach, to prophesy new philosophies and new sciences; to make, to give, to live.

I believe that the keynote of life is work, and that upon the honesty of work depends all that is worthy and lasting in art and in life.

G. S.

PRACTICAL CRAFTSMAN CEMENT HOUSE PLANNED FOR BEAUTY AND CONVENIENCE

IN the houses shown in this book we have endeavored to embody certain features essential to beauty and usefulness, the important elements for which every homemaker is seeking, the happy blending of which will create that homelike quality desired by whoever contemplates building. The usefulness of a house depends upon the arrangement of the space enclosed within its outer walls, and in designing Craftsman houses the floor plans receive first attention. From these the remainder of the house is worked out. The exterior thus becomes the outward expression of the inner purpose.

A study of the floor plans of the cement house which we have shown on pages 12 and 13, will serve to illustrate how close is the relation between a practical arrangement of rooms and a comfortable and beautiful home. The approach to the living room is an especially interesting feature. In addition to the recessed porch, which always gives a peculiarly intimate sense of inner seclusion and comfort, there is a little hall with an inviting window seat facing the stairway. The first view of the living room is stamped with the genial welcome of the open fireplace and the convenient proximity of the well-chosen fireside friends—the books. A good book and a glowing hearth are closely associated in the minds of most home-loving people, and it is fitting that they should be allowed an intimate alliance in the plan of the house.

The perspective drawing of the living room gives some idea of the decorative quality which results from a careful handling of the structural features of the interior. The ornamental use of Tapestry brick in the chimney-piece, the frank simplicity which characterizes the beams and woodwork, the treatment of the windows, and the placing of the staircase so that one gets a glimpse of its simple construction through the wide living room entrance, as well as from the dining room, all these things combine to form a quiet and dignified background for the more personal furnishings of the house. The convenient placing of the dining room in relation to the kitchen and to the living room, and the placing of the kitchen where the odors of the coming meal will not reach the waiting guests long before the meal is served, are in keeping with the rest of the carefully considered plan. A secluded dining porch is to be seen within easy access of the kitchen, so that during summer months meals could be served there with little additional work.

Upstairs the arrangement is as simple as it is compact, four good-sized bedrooms, a bathroom, and plenty of closet room being provided. The square space at the end of the upper hallway, directly above the lower entrance, could be used as a tiny sewing room, or it could be transformed into a most inviting nook with a comfortably cushioned window seat.

Cement on metal lath was chosen for the construction of this house, because these materials have proven themselves to be both durable and inexpensive. Though the original cost is more, the continued necessity for repairs is done away with, which makes it cheaper in the end. The lines of the building, as projected from the floor plans, lend themselves especially to the use of cement or concrete, for they are essentially simple. There is a decorative quality in this severe simplicity of line, and any possibility of severity being

CEMENT HOUSE, WITH SEVEN ROOMS AND DINING PORCH

Published in The Craftsman, December, 1911.

CRAFTSMAN CEMENT HOUSE: NO. 12

carried to extreme is obviated by the grouping of the small-paned, double-hung windows, and by the use of vines about the chimney and pillars of the porches, and by the plants at the base of the walls. The stone chimneys add an element of picturesqueness to the exterior, and the Ruberoid roof, which may be red or green as preferred, is pleasantly broken

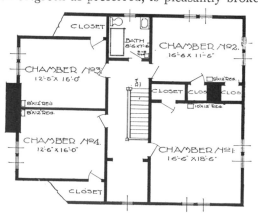

CEMENT HOUSE NO. 125: FIRST FLOOR PLAN.

HOUSE NO. 125: SECOND FLOOR PLAN.

by the long dormer which allows ample height for the rooms of the upper story.

The rooms on the first floor may be finished in stained chestnut, and the floors may be maple finished with vinegar and iron rust, which gives a rich tone to the whole room. The entire upper part of the house may be finished in red gumwood, with maple floors.

Important and interesting features of the house are the Craftsman fireplace-furnaces, which are so constructed that they not only furnish the joy and companionship of an open fire, but heat and ventilate the whole house as well.

In furnishing this house various Craftsman fittings could be used that would harmonize with the treatment of the interior as well as add to its comfort. In the living room, for instance, we have shown two lanterns from the Craftsman workshops, the design of which is

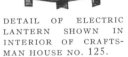

DETAIL OF ELECTRIC LANTERN SHOWN IN INTERIOR OF CRAFTSMAN HOUSE NO. 125.

illustrated more clearly in a detail cut. These ceiling lights could be supplemented by a bracket lantern such as the one shown here, which could be fastened to the wall at any convenient height.

In the wide openings between the entrance and the living room and dining room, portières could of course be hung to obviate any possibility of draft from the front door, adding at the same time to the general comfort of the interior and securing a greater sense of privacy. These hangings would also serve to soften the straight lines of the woodwork, and would naturally carry out, in color and design, the decorative scheme of the rooms.

CRAFTSMAN ELECTRIC BRACKET LANTERN.

Long, comfortably cushioned seats might also be placed in the living room on each side of the fireplace—one against the wall at the left, and the other beneath the windows. These would contribute much to the homelike quality of the place, and would transform that end of the room into a sort of inglenook. Or, a long settle might be placed directly in front of the hearth, with a table of the same length at the back so that the light from a reading lamp would fall over one's shoulder at a convenient angle. In fact, the room affords many possibilities of arrangement, and the details could be planned according to personal taste.

LIVING ROOM IN HOUSE NO. 125, SHOWING FIREPLACE-FURNACE AND GLIMPSE OF STAIRWAY.

CEMENT HOUSE SHOWING INTERESTING ROOF TREATMENT AND ROOMY HOMELIKE INTERIOR

Published in The Craftsman, November, 1909.

CRAFTSMAN CEMENT HOUSE WITH EIGHT ROOMS AND THREE PORCHES: NO. 79.

LONG, sloping roofs of shingle or slate, in which dormers are broken out to give the necessary height to the chambers, make the exterior of this cement house especially charming. The building is strongly constructed upon truss metal laths, and every care has been taken to avoid the possibility of leakage. The cement is brought close about the windows, which are so grouped as to break the wall into pleasing spaces.

The rooms are fitted with ample closets and are well lighted with large windows, both casement and double-hung. The amount of furniture that is built into the house will make quite a difference in the expense of furnishing it. In the kitchen there is a long dresser and a sink fitted with drip boards. A sideboard, flanked by china closets, is built into the dining room beneath the group of five small casements. The living room shows a long seat beneath the front windows, with built-in bookshelves on either side, and seats beside the piano in the opposite wall; but the most attractive feature is the deep inglenook which runs out between the twin porches that are connected with the room by means of

CEMENT HOUSE   NO. 79.

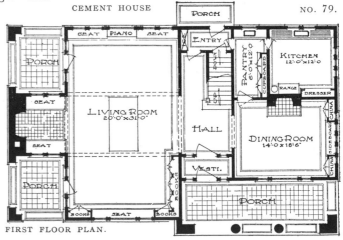

FIRST FLOOR PLAN.

14

CEMENT HOUSE, WITH EIGHT ROOMS AND THREE PORCHES

long glass doors. The chimneypiece is of split field stone with rough tile hearth. On either side are two long settles with high wainscoted backs splayed out a little for greater comfort, and casement windows above. The ceiling within the nook is lower than that of the living room, being dropped to a level with the top of the heavy lintel across the entrance, adding a greater air of seclusion. From this lintel could be suspended Craftsman lanterns of hammered copper with amber glass. The nook, in fact, affords many opportunities for those little individual touches, in color, texture and detail, which can bring such comfort and beauty into an interior. And when the firelight plays over the warm tones of the woodwork and the soft varied colors of the stone, glinting upon a bit of metal above the mantelpiece, or upon the brighter colors of the cushions, the inglenook becomes truly the heart of the house, the center of interest of the home.

Turning to the floor plan of the upper story, we find that this is also worth studying, for it shows an unusually pleasant arrangement of the bedrooms. These are all light and airy,

and the windows, with their small panes, add greatly to the charm of the interior, and at the same time give a decorative touch to the outer walls. The most attractive feature of this plan is the built-in window seats which are seen in little nooks in four of the bedrooms, and which add so much to the comfort and cheerfulness of the rooms. The various corners, moreover, that break up the walls afford unique possibilities of furnishing.

VIEW OF THE FIREPLACE NOOK IN THE LIVING ROOM, SHOWING CHIMNEY-PIECE OF SPLIT FIELD STONE, ROUGH TILE HEARTH AND SETTLES WITH WAINSCOTED BACKS ON EITHER SIDE.

15

THREE-STORY CRAFTSMAN BUNGALOW SUITABLE FOR A HILLSIDE SITE

Published in The Craftsman, January, 1911.

THREE-STORY BUNGALOW FOR HILLSIDE SITE: NO. 105.

A THREE-STORY bungalow is unusual, yet the Craftsman house illustrated here shows a distinct bungalow form of construction. Stone is used for the foundation and lower walls, cement for the walls above, boards for the gable, and slates for the roof. The main floor contains the kitchen, living room and two bedrooms, with room in the attic for three additional bedrooms if required. The basement is divided into a large billiard room, laundry, furnace and fuel room, and storeroom, so that, although the house does not look very large, there is really a great deal of space in it.

As pictured here, the house is built upon irregular ground, so that the foundation wall varies in height. The entrance to the house is approached by a terrace which leads to the square entrance porch. At the opposite side a straight road runs directly into the garage, which occupies all the space under the porch that is sheltered by the pergola. This placing of the garage is specially convenient, as it not only gives the best possible shelter to the motor car, but enables its occupants to descend within the house itself—a great advantage in stormy weather—and to go directly into the billiard room, from which a stairway leads up to the living room. The garage is fourteen feet broad, giving ample room for the motor car and also for a workbench, which is placed just below the line of casement windows. The billiard room, which is very large, is lighted by the three groups of casement windows that appear in the lower wall at the front of the house. A large fireplace in the middle of the

THREE-STORY BUNGALOW FOR HILLSIDE SITE

BUILT-IN SIDEBOARD, CLOSETS, WINDOW SEAT, DESK AND BOOKSHELVES IN LIVING ROOM OF HOUSE NO. 105.

opposite wall gives warmth and cheer to the room, and its construction is sufficiently rugged to allow a bold and rather primitive form of decoration and furnishing, suitable to such a basement playroom for men. The interior view given below may be helpful in its suggestion of the corner seat, willow chair, and Craftsman hanging and bracket lights. Just back of the billiard room is seen the very convenient arrangement of the stairway, which has a double landing, giving a means of communication between the living room and the billiard room

and also between the kitchen and the furnace room. This lies just behind the fireplace, and the coal cellar joins it. The oblong space in the corner is not excavated, nor is the corresponding space at the corner of the billiard room; but if more room were required in the basement it would be an easy matter to excavate and utilize these spaces. The laundry is a square room large enough to hold the necessary conveniences for washing.

On the main floor the entrance leads directly into the large living room, one end of which is

CORNER OF BILLIARD ROOM ON GROUND FLOOR OF THREE-STORY CRAFTSMAN BUNGALOW NO. 105.

17

THREE-STORY BUNGALOW FOR HILLSIDE SITE

to be used as a dining room. A glass door from this end opens upon the porch that is covered by the pergola, and another leads to the dining porch, which is roofed in so that it may be used in all moderately warm weather,

CRAFTSMAN BUNGALOW.   NO. 105.

GROUND FLOOR PLAN.

whether stormy or not. A large fireplace, with a massive chimneypiece, occupies the center of the inner wall space, the staircase being placed on one side and the doors leading to the kitchen and the dining porch upon the other. The entire front of the long room, although treated as a unit, contains three separate built-in features. In the center is a large window seat occupying the space below the main group of windows. At one side of this is a large built-in writing desk, with bookshelves on either side and double windows above, and on the other side, in the part of the room that is meant to be used as a dining room, is a built-in sideboard with china closets. Treated in this way, the whole end of the room is made interesting and decorative, while it serves all purposes of utility and convenience. There is opportunity for a generous display of woodwork, and the line of wainscoting that runs around the whole room is preserved unbroken by the tops of the bookshelves, china closets and the high ends and back of the window seat.

According to this arrangement there is ample space left on the main floor for two bedrooms with the necessary closet room at the end of the house just back of the entrance porch. A bathroom occupies the square space in rear of the stairs and the kitchen is placed directly

behind the big fireplace in the living room, so that the flue may be utilized for the kitchen range, thus doing away with the necessity for a second chimney. The service porch, pantry and ice-box form an extension at the back of the house. In case a different arrangement is preferred, the space given to the two bedrooms and the bath could easily be used for a workroom, a library or den, as the three bedrooms in the attic would be enough to accommodate a small family.

These three rooms are of good size and are well lighted and ventilated. Plenty of space is given to closets, and there is also a bathroom. Our own idea was to have these upper bedrooms serve for guest rooms and possibly a servant's room, leaving the two rooms on the main floor for the family; but, of course, the necessities of each individual case would dictate the details of the arrangement.

FIRST FLOOR PLAN.

BUNGALOW NO. 105.

SECOND FLOOR PLAN: NO. 105.

18

CRAFTSMAN CEMENT DWELLING INSPIRED BY OLD-FASHIONED NEW ENGLAND FARMHOUSE

Published in The Craftsman, September, 1909.

CRAFTSMAN CEMENT FARMHOUSE: NO. 74.

ALTHOUGH built according to a very modern method—cement on metal lath—this building will be seen to follow the salient structural features of the so-called New England farmhouse, varied, however, by the big dormer which breaks the long, sloping roof at the back to admit more light and air to the second story. The four-foot overhang at the eaves, with the deep brackets that support it, the large cement chimneys at either end, the porch at the corner and the pergola over the front door give interest to the exterior.

This pergola is better seen in the detail view of the building, on the next page. Instead of using the customary single heavy beam in the roof supports, we have shown here two smaller beams, thus making a lighter structure while taking nothing away from the strength of it. The pillars are of cement. The vine over the pergola and the flower-boxes set between the pillars add a note of grace and hospitality to the entrance, and seem to knit the house more closely to its surroundings. Vines could also be grown at the sides of the house, to soften

the long straight lines of the two chimneys.

The entrance door, with its long metal hinges and knocker, and its row of small lights in the upper part of the panels, is as simple as it is decorative, and is quite in keeping with the rest of the construction. The casements on either side of the door serve to light the hall within, and at the same time add another note of welcome to the exterior.

The interior of the house, of course, meets the modern standards of comfort. The placing of the stairs, however, suggests the old New England arrangement; the landing is raised only a few steps above the living room and a railing runs along its edge so that the effect of a balcony is given. From the landing the stairs continue to the second story behind a partition of spindles, making them a part of both living room and hall, thus turning a necessary feature of the house into a most artistic one.

The large living room is well lighted by the window groups at the front and rear, and by the two large windows on each side of the

CRAFTSMAN CEMENT FARMHOUSE

DETAIL VIEW OF CRAFTSMAN CEMENT FARMHOUSE NO. 74, SHOWING FRONT ENTRANCE WITH CEMENT PILLARS AND PERGOLA CONSTRUCTION ABOVE. THE SIMPLE BUT EFFECTIVE TREATMENT OF THE DOOR AND SMALL CASEMENTS ON EITHER SIDE IS ALSO WORTH NOTICING.

CRAFTSMAN CEMENT FARMHOUSE

fireplace. A glass door leads onto the sheltered porch at the back, where meals may be served whenever the weather is warm enough. This porch also connects with the dining

HOUSE NO. 74:
FIRST FLOOR
PLAN.

room, which is provided with a built-in sideboard and communicates with the kitchen through a convenient pantry. The kitchen, it will be noticed, has ready access to the staircase, hall and entrance door. In fact the arrangement and relation of all the rooms has been made as simple and direct as possible in order to facilitate the work of housekeeping.

In one corner of the hall a coat closet is provided, and a wide opening at the right leads into a little den or library. In here is another open fireplace which utilizes the same chimney as the kitchen range, and on either side of the chimneypiece are built-in bookcases.

The upper floor plan gives one a sense of compactness and spaciousness combined. The rooms are large and airy, and amply supplied with closets. Two of the front bedrooms have built-in window seats—a feature which always adds much to the comfort and charm of an interior—and the bedroom to the right has the additional attraction of an open fire-

place which uses the same chimney as that of the den below. The large chamber on the left communicates with a sleeping porch at the rear which, being sheltered on three sides, is protected from the weather, and could be used practically the year round by those who believe in the healthfulness of outdoor sleeping. The large bedroom also communicates with the smaller central bedroom in front, which can also be entered from the hall. This little bedroom could be used as a dressing room, if desired, in connection with the adjoining room at the left. The bathroom is large and is provided with a linen closet.

All through the house, it will be noticed, in both the exterior and the interior, there is an entire absence of affectation or superfluous ornament. The treatment of the whole is extremely simple, and whatever decorative quality the building and the rooms possess will be found to be the outcome of necessary elements of the construction, handled in such a manner as to combine practical architectural features with comfort and usefulness of arrangement and harmony of proportion and line. Like all the houses shown here, the plans could be adapted to meet individual requirements.

HOUSE
NO. 74:

SECOND
FLOOR
PLAN.

21

SIMPLE CEMENT COTTAGE FOR A SMALL FAMILY

Published in The Craftsman, June, 1910.

SIMPLE CEMENT CRAFTSMAN COTTAGE: NO. 91.

A SMALL cement cottage is illustrated here such as we find coming more and more into favor as the possibilities of this excellent building material are developed. The compact floor plans, which are practically square, result in a very simple exterior. The walls and foundation of this house are built of cement on metal lath, and the

hood over the entrance door is of the same material. The shape and structure of this hood express the limitations and possibilities of cement, and reveal the method of construction as frankly as do the beams and brackets used in wood construction. The severity of the plain cement walls is relieved by the grouping and placing of the windows, and by the use of wide V-jointed boards in the gables, the lower ends of

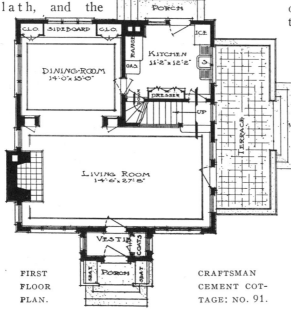

FIRST FLOOR PLAN.

CRAFTSMAN CEMENT COTTAGE: NO. 91.

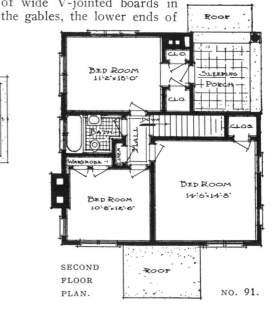

SECOND FLOOR PLAN.

NO. 91.

CEMENT COTTAGE FOR A SMALL FAMILY

the boards resting against a wide beam that marks the upper termination of the cement wall. The roof is of Ruberoid, the lengths of the material being brought down from the ridge-pole to the heavy roll at the eaves, and each joint being covered with a strip of wood which caps the rafter to which the roofing is fastened.

A cement seat is built at either side of the entrance porch, and the front door opens into a small vestibule with a coat closet at one end. This vestibule leads directly into the living room, which extends across the entire front of the house, with a big fireplace at one end and a glass door at the other leading to the terrace at the side. This living room is wainscoted to the height of the frieze with wide V-jointed boards.

The staircase and landing occupy the greater part of the wall between the living room and kitchen, and the remainder of the wall space is taken up by the wide opening into the dining room. This is finished in the same way as the living room, as the intention is to throw the two into one large room, the division between them being merely suggested. The entire end of the dining room is taken up by a built-in sideboard, with a group of three casement windows set high in the wall above,

and a good-sized china closet on either side.

The kitchen is arranged to simplify housework as much as possible.

The upper floor is divided into three bedrooms, a bathroom, plenty of closets, and a good-sized sleeping porch which can be screened in summer and glassed in winter if desired. The bathroom and this sleeping porch, as well as the terrace below, may be floored with cement.

This cottage admits of the use of many interesting furnishings and fixtures, such as the lamp fitted to the newel-post of the staircase in the view of the living room shown below. This lamp, which comes in hammered copper or wrought iron, with amber glass, seems especially in keeping with the general treatment of the interior, and while simple in design, is decorative as well as useful.

DETAIL OF NEWEL-POST LAMP SHOWN IN INTERIOR VIEW OF HOUSE NO. 91.

CORNER OF LIVING ROOM IN CRAFTSMAN CEMENT COTTAGE NO. 91, SHOWING STAIRCASE WITH NEWEL-POST LAMP, AND DOOR LEADING ONTO THE TERRACE AT THE SIDE OF THE HOUSE.

INEXPENSIVE ONE-STORY BUNGALOW WITH EFFECTIVE USE OF TRELLIS

Published in The Craftsman, September, 1911.   CEMENT AND CLAPBOARD ONE-STORY BUNGALOW: NO. 123.

ONE END OF THE LIVING ROOM IN BUNGALOW NO. 123, SHOWING CRAFTSMAN FIREPLACE-FURNACE WITH DECORATIVE USE OF TAPESTRY BRICK.

24

CEMENT AND CLAPBOARD ONE-STORY BUNGALOW

PLANNED for a small family and designed for a narrow suburban lot, this little bungalow may be inexpensively and yet substantially built. Cement plaster with boarded gable and slate roof are the materials shown here, although concrete foundation and shingled sides and roof might be used; but the durability of cement would more than compensate for its greater initial cost.

The veranda floor may be of concrete, and the pillars of concrete or rough hand-hewn logs. The trellis and the pergola entrance add a decorative note which is pleasing both before the vines have grown and when they are leafless during winter.

The floor plan shows a small but comfortable interior, comprising a large sitting room to be used as a dining room, and two bedrooms, a bathroom and kitchen. Ample closet space is allowed and the kitchen is equipped with all the necessary conveniences. The bungalow can be well warmed and ventilated by the centrally located Craftsman fireplace-furnace, the illustration of which shows an effective use of Tapestry brick.

On each side of this fireplace, with its decorative chimney and tiled hearth, are paneled doors, one of which leads into the kitchen, and the other into the hall. Each door has small square lights set in the upper portion, and these, together with the well-balanced groups of windows in the front and side walls, add to the structural interest of the room. The simple treatment of the woodwork, while possessing a certain decorative quality, will form a restful and unobtrusive background for the furnishings. The built-in window seats in the nooks formed by the vestibule will also prove welcome features of the interior.

A similar seat is seen in the recess between the closets in one of the bedrooms, with small windows above it overlooking the porch. The other bedroom is also a fair size and is well lighted by windows at the back and side. The small hallway, with its closet in one corner, takes up as little space as possible, and communicates with each room of the bungalow.

The plan of the house is one which lends itself to a light form of housekeeping, and if simply furnished the work of the household could be reduced to a minimum.

The porch, being recessed and sheltered on two sides, would serve as a pleasant outdoor living room during warm weather, and it could be glassed in during the winter if de-

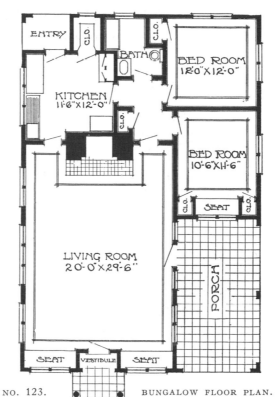

NO. 123.   BUNGALOW FLOOR PLAN.

sired,—an arrangement which would add considerably to the space within the bungalow. In any case, it could be easily furnished with a few willow pieces,—chairs, table and swinging seat with comfortable cushions,—and if screened from the street in summer by a plentiful growth of vines, it would be a very serviceable as well as a very charming feature of the house.

ANDIRONS OF WROUGHT IRON WHICH MIGHT BE USED ON THE OPEN HEARTH IN ANY CRAFTSMAN INTERIOR.

SMALL ONE-STORY CEMENT BUNGALOW WITH SLATE ROOF, DESIGNED FOR A NARROW LOT

Published in The Craftsman, September, 1911.

CEMENT BUNGALOW FOR NARROW LOT: NO. 124

THIS one-story bungalow is a small, simply-arranged dwelling, intended for a narrow lot, and planned economically to afford the greatest possible comfort within a limited space. Cement plaster would be suitable for the walls and slate for the roof.

The most attractive feature of the exterior is the long porch which extends across the front of the house. This is enclosed by a low parapet of cement from which rise the hewn log pillars which support the pergola roof. Against this parapet is placed trelliswork, and from the trellis vines may be trained up the pillars and over the beams of the pergola above. Thus a very pleasant entrance will be formed, and even in winter, when the vines are leafless, the trelliswork and pergola construction overhead will still lend a distinctly decorative note to the exterior, softening by their graceful details the severity of what would otherwise be a plain cement building.

A touch of interest is also given to the side of the house by the extension of the main roof over the kitchen entrance, with its vine-encircled pillars rising from the cement floor.

Since the use of trelliswork is found to hold such charm, it might even be carried out further, and used in the entrance to the garden at the front of the house. The line drawing shown here gives a suggestion for such treatment, which would make a very effective gateway and would link the house more closely to its surroundings. Another factor in relieving the plainness of the bungalow walls is the use of small panes in all the windows. This not only breaks up the surface in a pleasing way, but at the same time seems to carry out the effect of the trelliswork.

The front door opens from the pergola porch directly into the ample living room, which is well lighted by the groups of windows on three sides, and is provided with an open fireplace. The latter, if a Craftsman fireplace-furnace, will serve to heat and ventilate the entire bungalow.

The kitchen and two bedrooms, though of moderate dimensions, will be large enough for a small family, and the whole plan is one that will lend itself to simple housekeeping.

The illustration of one of the rooms in this

CEMENT BUNGALOW FOR A NARROW LOT

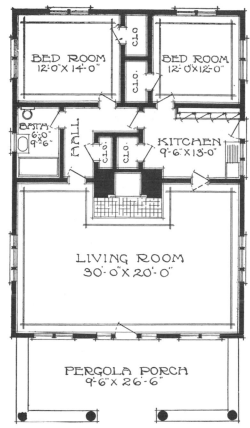

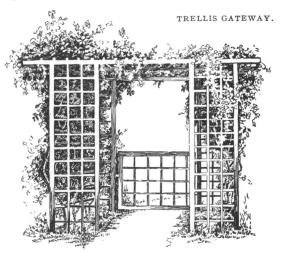

TRELLIS GATEWAY.

FLOOR PLAN OF BUNGALOW NO. 124.

bungalow will give some impression of the effective simplicity of Craftsman bedroom furniture. The plain lines and restful proportions of the bed and bureau are thoroughly in keeping with the treatment of the woodwork, and the small square lights set in the paneled door form a pleasant relief to the flat surface of the walls. In the interior of this bungalow, as in other Craftsman houses, it will be found that much of the interest comes from the thoughtful handling of necessary architectural details, and the more carefully these are worked out, the easier will be the task of furnishing the home.

BEDROOM IN CEMENT BUNGALOW, NO. 124, WITH CRAFTSMAN FURNITURE.

CEMENT HOUSE WITH PERGOLA, SLEEPING BAL-
CONY AND PRACTICAL INTERESTING INTERIOR

Published in The Craftsman, September, 1910.

CRAFTSMAN TWO-STORY CEMENT HOUSE WITH EIGHT ROOMS AND RECESSED SLEEPING BALCONY: NO. 97.

THIS cement house is simply built, with a low-pitched roof showing a wide over-hang. The roof is Ruberoid stretched over the rafters and battened down as usual, but instead of the roll at the eaves we have brought it down to the inside of the cypress gutter. The rafters are hollowed out, and the gutter let into the curve so that it DIAGRAM OF CYPRESS forms a continuous trough, GUTTER USED IN as shown in the diagram. HOUSE NO. 97. The pergola in front is sup-ported on massive cement pillars, and the timber con-struction above is orna-mental as well as sturdy and enduring. Over this pergola is a partly recessed sleeping porch, ending in a balcony that is supported on the extended timbers of the second floor. A group of six windows and a glass door in the back of this porch give plenty of light to the bedroom which opens upon it.

The living room extends across the whole

front of the house, and at one end is a large chimneypiece extending to the ceiling, the space on either side being filled with book-cases. A square den opens out of the living room at one side of the staircase, and at the other side is the dining room with a second fireplace flanked with combination sideboards and china closets.

This house has one bedroom on the lower floor with a small private bath attached. On the second floor is a large square bathroom, and the closets also are unusually big. Two large storerooms are provided.

CEMENT HOUSE WITH EIGHT ROOMS AND SLEEPING BALCONY

FIRST FLOOR PLAN: NO. 97.   SECOND FLOOR PLAN: NO. 97.

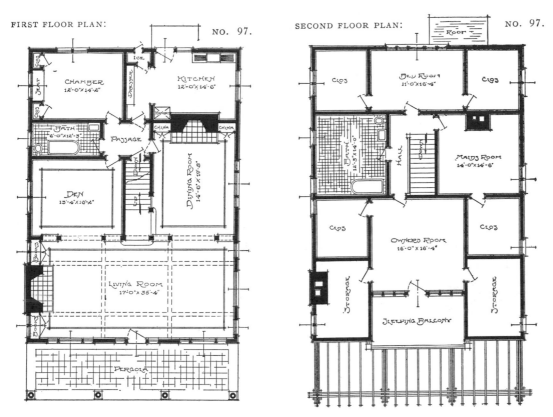

END OF DINING ROOM IN HOUSE NO. 97, SHOWING FIREPLACE AND BUILT-IN CHINA CLOSETS.

PLASTER DWELLING FOR TOWN OR COUNTRY

Published in The Craftsman, January, 1909.   PLASTER HOUSE WITH TYPICAL CRAFTSMAN INTERIOR: NO. 58.

THE house shown here is suitable for either an ordinary lot in a town or village, or for the open country. It has plastered or stuccoed walls, foundation of field stone, and shingled roof. The design, however, lends itself quite as readily to shingled or clapboarded walls.

The outside kitchen at the back is recommended only in the event of the house being built in the country, because in town it would hardly be needed.

The plan of the lower story shows the usual Craftsman arrangement of rooms opening into

STONE FIREPLACE AND BUILT-IN BOOKCASES IN LIVING ROOM OF HOUSE NO. 58.

PLASTER HOUSE WITH TYPICAL CRAFTSMAN INTERIOR

one another with only suggested divisions. The entrance door opens into a small entry, screened by portières from the living room so that no draught from the front door is felt inside. On the outside wall of the living room is the arrangement of fireplace and bookcases, as shown in the detail illustration. The chimneypiece is built of split field stone laid up in cement and runs clear to the ceiling. A bookcase is built in on either side and above each one of these are two small double-hung windows. The tops of the bookcases serve admirably as shelves for plants.

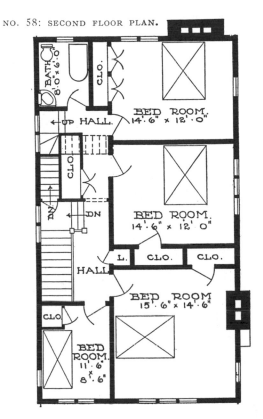

HOUSE NO. 58:   FIRST FLOOR PLAN.

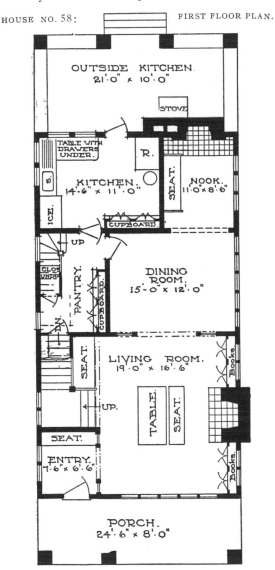

In the center of the room may be placed a large table with a settle of exactly the same length placed back to it and facing the fire, so that it affords an ideal arrangement for anyone who wishes to sit facing the fire with the light from a reading lamp falling over the shoulder. The back of the seat would be on a level or a little below the top of the table, so that the two seem almost to be one piece of furniture. This is usually found to be a pleasant and comfortable arrangement.

The dining room is simply a continuation of the living room, from which it is divided only by posts and panels with open spaces in the upper part, as shown in the illustration of the fireplace. Beyond this dining room again is a nook, the end of which is completely filled by a large fireplace using the same chimney as the kitchen range and the stove in the outside kitchen. The seat in this nook is not built in, but a broad bench or settle would be very comfortable if placed as suggested in the plan.

The kitchen though not large is compactly planned, and the work is greatly simplified by the small space and convenient arrangement.

31

COMMODIOUS CEMENT HOUSE WITH TERRACE, PORCHES AND SLEEPING BALCONIES

Published in The Craftsman, August, 1910.

CRAFTSMAN CEMENT HOUSE: NO. 95.

HERE is a substantial and moderate-sized cement house. The lines are all rather straight and severe, the pillars and parapets being plain and the walls broken only by the groups of windows. All look of bareness in the upper part of the house is taken away by the effect of the widely overhanging roof with its exposed rafters, heavy beams and the large brackets which support it. The roof itself is of Ruberoid, finished at the eaves with a wood gutter. Below, the square outline of the house is broken by a veranda that is partly open to the sky and partly roofed in. This veranda may be floored with red cement marked off in squares, and in front has much the appearance of a terrace, as it is shielded only by a low parapet crowned with flower-boxes. At either side of the house the veranda is sheltered by a roof which forms the floor of the sleeping balcony above. These balconies are also shielded by para-

pets surmounted with flower-boxes, so that the cots or low beds are concealed from view. The balconies are open to the sky, but could be covered with awnings if desired. The exposed win-

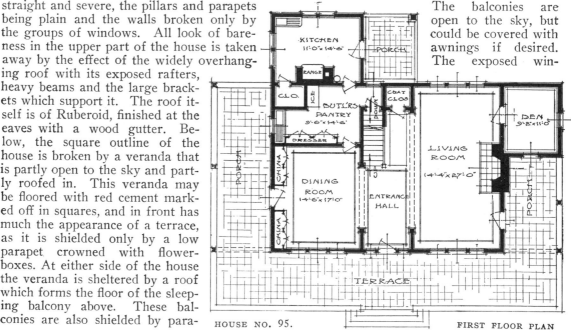

HOUSE NO. 95.

FIRST FLOOR PLAN

32

COMMODIOUS CRAFTSMAN CEMENT HOUSE

dows and entrance door are sheltered by cement hoods constructed like the walls and extending outward in a graceful sweep that not only protects the windows and door, but adds a distinctly decorative feature to the walls. These hoods are supported upon heavy timber brackets. Beneath the balconies the timber construction is left exposed as it is in the roof.

The house is arranged in the typical Craftsman way, the entrance hall being merely suggested as a division between the dining room and living room. As a matter of fact, the whole lower part of the house is open, with the exception of the kitchen and pantry at the back and the den at one side of the living room. The staircase, although apparently in the entrance hall, is really a part of the living room, which is divided from the hall only by a massive overhead beam. There is a coat closet in one corner and plenty of space for a built-in seat in the recess formed by the stairway. The living room is very plain as regards woodwork and other finish, but if the wood be properly selected and treated the room will have a greater beauty than could be

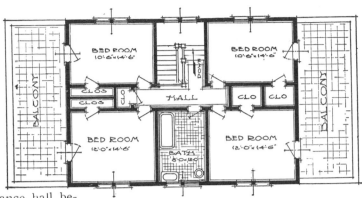

HOUSE NO. 95: SECOND FLOOR PLAN

given by a more elaborate arrangement. The walls are wainscoted with wide V-jointed boards to the height of the frieze, and the big square chimneypiece of Tapestry brick extends only to the same line, which thus runs unbroken all around the room. Above this line the chimneypiece is plastered like the ceiling and frieze with rough sand-finished plaster, tinted to harmonize with the woodwork.

On the opposite side of the entrance hall is the dining room, lighted in front with a group of windows like that in the living room. A glass door opens on the porch and on either side of this door are china closets.

TAPESTRY BRICK FIREPLACE IN LIVING ROOM OF CRAFTSMAN CEMENT HOUSE NO. 95.

33

CEMENT HOUSE, COMPACT YET SPACIOUS, SUITABLE FOR A CITY STREET

Published in The Craftsman, May, 1909.

TEN-ROOM CEMENT HOUSE: NO. 66.

CORNER OF LIVING ROOM IN HOUSE NO. 66, WITH SUGGESTION FOR PLACING OF TABLE AND FIRESIDE SEAT.

TEN-ROOM CEMENT HOUSE SUITABLE FOR A CITY STREET

THIS house is built entirely of cement on a stone foundation, and requires a frontage of not less than fifty feet. The entrance of the porch is roofed over and the rest is pergola construction.

The cement chimney, which is built in three widths, forms an interesting variation at the side of the house, and the grouping of the windows with their large and small panes helps to break up the plain cement surface into well-proportioned spaces, while adding at the same time to the charm of the interior.

The interior view shows casement windows in the dining room and above the built-in bookcases on each side of the living-room fireplace. The chimneypiece is built of rough bricks of varied colors,—old blue, burnt sienna, dull yellow and many tan and salmon shades, and when rightly arranged the result is beautiful, especially if the colors are repeated in the decorative scheme of the room. The shelf is

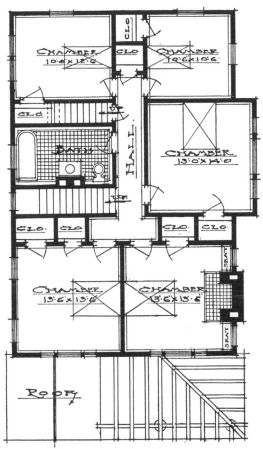

HOUSE NO. 66: SECOND FLOOR PLAN.

a thick board, of whatever wood is selected for the finishing of the room.

The dining room is wainscoted and is separated only by narrow partitions from the living room. The sideboard is built in and the space between it and the rear wall is filled by a china closet. In the corresponding space between the sideboard and the front wall a swinging door leads into a roomy butler's pantry. The kitchen has several cupboards and also two big pantries, one of which contains the icebox. A few steps leading from a landing on the main stairway connect the kitchen with the upper part of the house. It will be noticed that the servant's sleeping room and bath are on the first floor. The large garret, which may be additionally lighted by skylights, would make a splendid billiard hall, or could be broken up into smaller rooms to be used for various purposes, such as storerooms or extra bedrooms.

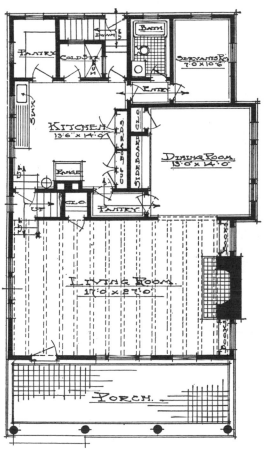

HOUSE NO. 66: FIRST FLOOR PLAN.

LARGE CEMENT HOUSE FOR TOWN OR COUNTRY

Published in The Craftsman, February, 1909.

CRAFTSMAN CEMENT HOUSE: NO. 60.

DESIGNED on simple lines that harmonize with almost any surroundings, this cement house is suitable for town, village or country site. The walls are of vitrified terra cotta blocks, the plastering being laid directly on the blocks both outside and inside. The foundation and parapet of the little terrace are of field stone.

Above the entrance door the wall runs up straight to the second story, where it terminates in a shallow balcony. Provision is made here for a flower-box, as the severity of the wall seems to demand the relief in color and line afforded by a cluster of plants and drooping vines. At the back of the house is a similar construction, for in place of a roof above the dining porch and part of the kitchen, is a large open balcony which may be used as a sleeping porch. This balcony is partially shielded by the cement parapet, but otherwise is open to the weather.

The roof, which has a wide overhang, is covered with rough heavy slates supported on strong beams and girders. The little roof over the bay window in the reception hall is also covered with slates and serves to break the straight lines of the wall. All the windows are casements and their grouping forms one of the distinctly decorative features of the construction.

The dining room opens with double glass doors upon the porch at the back of the

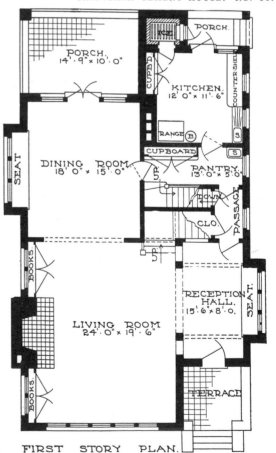

FIRST STORY PLAN.

36

LARGE CEMENT HOUSE FOR TOWN OR COUNTRY

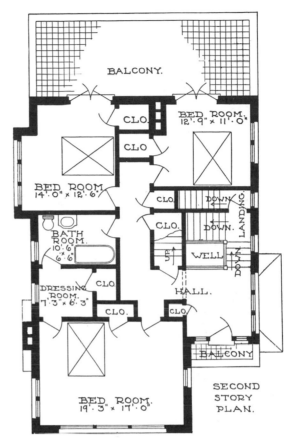

SECOND
STORY
PLAN.

house, which may be left open or screened in summer, and closed in winter for a dining porch or sun room. Built-in bookcases, wide inviting window seats and a big fireplace add to the comfort and structural interest of the rooms.

High wainscots are used throughout the reception hall, living room and dining room in this house, and the general effect of the divisions between the rooms and the arrangement of the staircase and landing is shown by the view of the interior given below. The woodwork in all these rooms would, of course, be the same, and the choice and treatment of it gives the keynote to the whole decorative scheme. Craftsman fittings, such as the hanging lanterns and newel-post lamp suggested here, seem especially appropriate.

The kitchen is compact and convenient, as are also the bedrooms, bathroom and closets on the second floor, and the little hall that opens out upon the balcony is admirably adapted for use as an upstairs sitting room. On the third floor are the billiard room and bedroom for the maid.

GLIMPSE OF ENTRANCE HALL AND STAIRCASE IN HOUSE NO. 60, AS SEEN FROM THE LIVING ROOM.

37

CONCRETE OR PLASTER HOUSE OF MODERATE SIZE AND SIMPLE DESIGN

Published in The Craftsman, February, 1910.

SIMPLY PLANNED CONCRETE OR PLASTER HOUSE WITH RECESSED ENTRANCE PORCH AND BALCONY: NO. 83.

EITHER concrete or plaster on metal lath may be used for this house, which is of moderate size, simply planned and comparatively inexpensive as to the cost of building. The severity of the straight lines and broad surfaces is relieved by the grouped windows, the arched openings of the entrance porch and the large dormer which occupies the inner angle of the L-shaped building.

No foundation is visible, the cement walls rising from a level with the ground. The chimneys are of concrete and the roof is covered with heavy rough slates which are much the same as the English flat tiles and which are not only fireproof and practically indestructible, but also give an admirable effect. The color of these slates would depend upon the color of the concrete walls. The slates come in gray, dull red, moss green and a variegated purplish tone, and upon the selection of the right color to blend with the walls and harmonize with the general tone of the landscape will depend much of the beauty of the house.

The wide low openings of the recessed entrance porch show a suggestion of the California Mission architecture in the flattened arches and massive concrete square pillars. The porch floor may be paved with Welsh quarries, or dull red cement marked off in squares, either material being durable, attractive and thoroughly in keeping with cement construction.

Perhaps the most individual of the exterior features is the group of dormer windows placed in the angle of the house. These serve to light and ventilate the two large bedrooms and the upper hall. A great part of the decorative effect of the windows of this house depends upon the use of rather small square panes and the grouping of the windows themselves in twos and threes in such a way as to give a massive rather than a scattered arrangement of openings in the wall.

The entrance door opens into a small vesti-

SIMPLY PLANNED HOUSE OF CONCRETE OR PLASTER

bule or entry which serves as a focal point for the arrangement of the rooms. The openings on either side are so broad as to leave only the merest suggestion of a partition, and the staircase may be regarded as a decorative structural feature common to both living room and dining room, rather than as a necessity to be relegated to the hall. This staircase leads up to a small square landing that is almost opposite the entrance door, and a door at the back of the open vestibule leads into a small enclosed passage which communicates with the kitchen and from which the stairs go down to the cellar.

Both living room and dining room are heated with large fireplaces, that in the dining room being placed

WILLOW CHAIR WHICH WOULD ADD TO THE COMFORT OF A CRAFTSMAN INTERIOR.

frieze at the top, while in the living room the walls might be of plaster divided into broad panels by stiles and plate rail of the same wood. The plaster would be most attractive if left rather rough and matt-finished in some pale tone.

On the upper floor the arrangement of rooms is much the same as it is below, three bedrooms occupying the same space as the living room, dining room and kitchen, with the bath directly over the pantry, and the hall a duplicate of the entry beneath. This makes a great saving in the cost of construction.

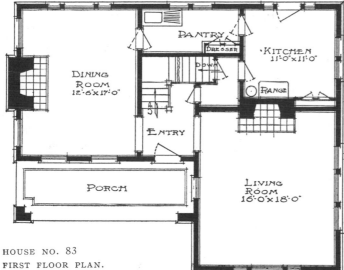

HOUSE NO. 83
FIRST FLOOR PLAN.

in the outside wall, while the one in the living room uses the same chimney as the kitchen range. We would suggest that the same woodwork and same general color scheme be used for the dining room and living room, thereby increasing the apparent space as well as the restfulness of the rooms. This does not at all imply monotony, for the same woodwork may be used in different ways and the arrangement of the wall spaces may convey a sense of variation that is interesting and yet entirely harmonious. For instance, if the woodwork were chestnut, dull-finished in a soft grayish brown, the dining room might be wainscoted high enough to leave only a plaster

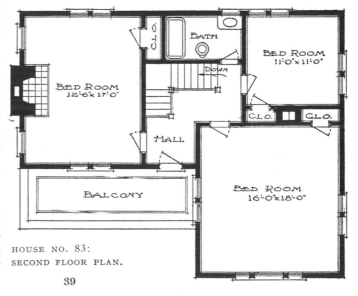

HOUSE NO. 83:
SECOND FLOOR PLAN.

39

INEXPENSIVE CEMENT AND SHINGLE COTTAGE

Published in The Craftsman, February, 1910.

THIS is a simple little house intended for a small family, and the plan has purposely been arranged so that the construction shall be as inexpensive as is compatible with durability and safety. The shingled roof has a steep pitch and its line is broken by two shallow dormers on either side which afford plenty of light to the bedrooms and add to the interest of the exterior. The walls of the lower story are of cement on metal lath and the upper walls are shingled. A very satisfactory effect could be obtained by giving a rough, pebble-dash finish to the cement and brushing on enough pigment to give it a tone of dull grayish green, varied by the inequalities in the surface of the cement. It would pay to use rived cypress shingles for the upper walls, as these are much more interesting and durable than the ordinary sawn shingles, and possess a surface that responds admirably to the treatment with diluted sulphuric acid which we have found most successful with this wood. The roof could be either moss green or grayish brown, a little darker than the shingles of the upper walls. Four heavy cement pillars support the roof of the porch, which is also of shingles the same color as the main roof of the house. The porch floor may

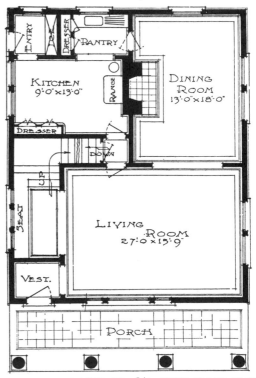

HOUSE NO. 84: FIRST FLOOR PLAN.

40

SEVEN-ROOM COTTAGE OF CEMENT AND SHINGLE

be paved with cement, or the outside edge might be plain cement of the same color as the walls, and the long strip down the center might be Welsh quarries or red cement marked off in squares.

The entrance door is at one end of the porch and opens into a small vestibule which leads directly into the living room, the opening being at right angles to the entrance door. A small partition separates the entrance from the stairway beyond, which is placed in a nook at the end of the living room. The entire end of this nook is occupied by a group of windows and a window seat. There is no fireplace in the living room, but in the dining room a large open fireplace uses the one central chimney which also serves for the kitchen range. The opening between the living room and the dining room is so broad that the fireplace serves equally well for both.

A small passageway leads from the kitchen to the living room, affording access to the entrance door, and in this passage is also the door leading to the cellar stairs. The kitchen is small and the pantry is little more than a nook in the larger room. Two large built-in china closets give plenty of room for the dishes, and the sink is placed in the pantry. Usually this arrangement would mean many additional steps, but the kitchen is so small that the distance from the range to the sink is no more than it would be in an ordinary room. An entry at the back of the kitchen communi-

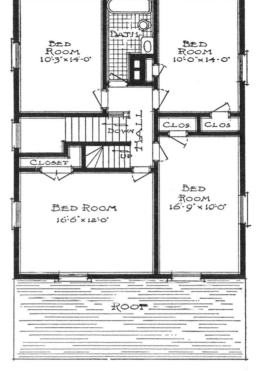

HOUSE NO. 84: SECOND FLOOR PLAN.

case in the center and the bathroom at the back.

On the whole, the interior of the cottage is one which would lend itself to simple housekeeping, and if tastefully furnished should prove both comfortable and attractive. The entrance could be made even more pleasant by the use of flower-boxes between the cement pillars of the porch, and vines planted along the side walls would add to the charm of the exterior and link the house more intimately to its surroundings.

The willow settle shown here would be a comfortable addition to this or any other interior, and would lighten up the general effect of the darker and heavier Craftsman oak furniture. The finish of soft green or deep golden brown would be a pleasant note in almost any color scheme, and the cushion coverings could be varied according to the material, color and design preferred.

LARGE WILLOW SETTLE WHICH HARMONIZES WELL WITH CRAFTSMAN OAK FURNITURE.

cates with a door leading to the outside, and furnishes a cool place for the ice box. A door from the pantry opens into the dining room.

The arrangement of the upper floor is very simple, as the four bedrooms occupy the four corners of the building with the hall and stair-

41

CRAFTSMAN HOUSE DESIGNED FOR NARROW LOT

Published in The Craftsman, May, 1909.
CEMENT AND SHINGLE HOUSE WITH SIX ROOMS, PORCHES AND BALCONY FOR NARROW LOT: NO. 67.

THIS cement and shingle house, being only nineteen feet wide, can be built on the ordinary town lot. It is as compact and comfortable as possible for winter use, and still not without certain advantages in spring and summer which are quite lacking in the usual town block. Front and rear porches and a balcony that may be shaded by an awning will do much toward making the summer heat endurable.

The lower story of the house is of cement on a low foundation of split field stone, and the second story is covered with hand-split shingles.

The suggestion of pergola at the rear of the house is merely a three-foot projection on a porch running under the second story and is built of the exposed timbers of the house supported by pillars. It not only adds to the attractiveness of that corner as seen from the street, but, covered with vines, would give a lovely outlook for the dining-room windows, and, since a door connects it with the kitchen, may be used itself as a dining room in warm weather.

The stone chimney, instead of running up at an even depth from the foundation to the roof and narrowing above the fireplace on the ground floor, keeps its same width almost to the eaves, but slants in at the second story to about half the original depth. This does away with the monotonous line of the ordinary outside chimney and gives a fireplace upstairs as wide, although not so deep, as the one on the ground floor.

All the exposed windows on the second story are hooded to protect them from driving storms. It is an attractive feature in the construction, especially in connection with the window group—a long French casement flanked on either side by a double-hung window, looking out upon the balcony. The floor of this balcony and the timbers that support it form the ceiling of the porch. The ends of these exposed supports, projecting beyond the beam on which they rest, emphasize the line between the porch and the balcony and are at once decorative and economical, for the open construction does away with much repairing of the sort occasioned by the action of dampness upon timbers sheathed in.

The entrance door, which is very simple in design, opens from the front porch directly into the large living hall. Here, on each side of the open fireplace, we find built-in book-

42

CEMENT AND SHINGLE HOUSE PLANNED FOR NARROW LOT

cases, with small casements set in the wall above. The room is also made light and cheerful by the window groups in the opposite wall and on each side of the entrance door, as well as by the wide opening into the dining room.

The view of the interior is made from a point just in front of the living room hearth and shows the use of spindles between the rooms and in the high balustrade that screens the two or three steps which lead up from the dining room, and are intended for the use of the servants. The meeting of these stairs with those from the living room makes an odd little corner that offers many possibilities for decorative effects. The dining room is wainscoted to the plate rail. The sideboard is built in and suggests the old-time dresser with its platter rail and side cupboards. There is a small pantry between the dining room and the kitchen, and the latter is fitted with the usual conveniences.

The upper floor plan shows a simple arrangement of the three bedrooms and bathroom.

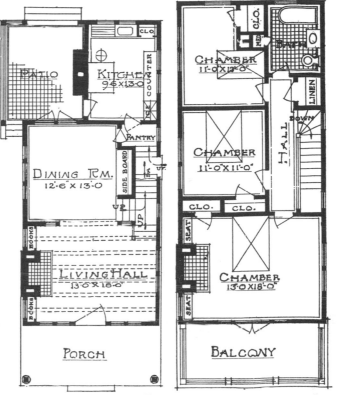

HOUSE NO. 67: FIRST AND SECOND FLOOR PLANS.

INTERIOR OF HOUSE NO. 67, SHOWING ONE CORNER OF THE LIVING HALL WITH GLIMPSE OF STAIRS AND DINING ROOM. THE DECORATIVE HANDLING OF WOODWORK AND STRUCTURAL FEATURES IS WORTH STUDYING.

SMALL TWO-STORY CEMENT HOUSE WITH RE-CESSED PORCH AND BALCONY

ALTHOUGH this house is a small one, its good proportions and the decorative quality of its structural features combine in producing a homelike and dignified impression. The severity of the building is broken by the recessed porch and sleeping balcony above, and the plain surfaces of the walls are relieved by the small hooded entrance and the design and

repeated in the balcony above, where they support the purlins that hold up the roof, thus carrying out the idea of massive construction in appearance as well as in actuality.

Much of the charm of this house would depend upon its color and the finish of the walls. The best effect would be gained by having the cement mixed with coarse brown sand and

Published in The Craftsman, March, 1910.

SEVEN-ROOM CEMENT HOUSE: NO. 85.

grouping of the windows. The walls are cement on metal lath—a form of construction which we have found most satisfactory—and the gables are sheathed with wide V-jointed boards which form a pleasant variation to the plainness of the cement below. The low-pitched roof, with its revealed rafters and purlins, offers no corners to collect moisture and induce rot under the action of the weather. The solid construction seen in the timbers is used in the hood over the entrance door. The round cement pillars of the lower porch are

simply troweled on without any other finish, rough or smooth. A beautiful color effect would be gained by giving the cement a soft indeterminate tone of brown that would blend with the brown wood tones of the boards in the gable and the shingles on the roof.

The porch and balcony, the living-room hearth, and also the bathroom might be paved with dull red cement. The shower bath in the corner of the bathroom is separated from the rest of the room by a partition like the outer walls extending part way to the ceiling.

44

SEVEN-ROOM CRAFTSMAN CEMENT HOUSE

The small entry at the corner of the house opens into the living room; the opening being at right angles to the entrance door in order to shut off the draught. The stair, which is separated from the entry by a partition, leads directly out of the living room, so that the first three steps and the landing form an attractive structural feature of the room. Between the staircase and the doorway leading into the small passageway to the kitchen, is a wide seat which is thus recessed from the main room. The spaces on either side of the chimneypiece are filled with built-in bookshelves.

Owing to the arrangement of this house, the living room and dining room are more definitely separated than is usual in a Craftsman interior. Both rooms are of the same size and are nearly square, and the arrangement

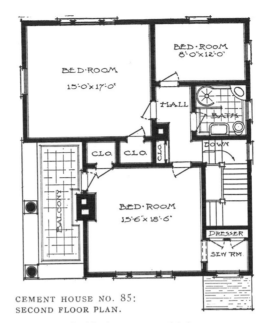

CEMENT HOUSE NO. 85:
SECOND FLOOR PLAN.

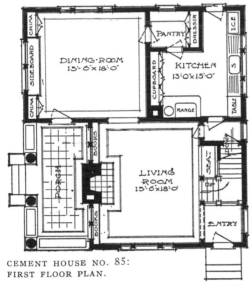

CEMENT HOUSE NO. 85:
FIRST FLOOR PLAN.

of chimneypiece and bookshelves in the living room is repeated by the built-in sideboard and china-cupboards that occupy the whole corresponding side of the dining room. The door from the dining room leads to the porch, where the table may be set in warm weather, and which provides a pleasant outdoor sitting room. There is no direct communication between the dining room and the kitchen, but swing doors from both rooms lead into the pantry, which occupies a corner of the space allotted to the kitchen. The kitchen itself is small, but very conveniently arranged, with cupboards, table, dressers, etc.

As the plan shows, the furnishing of the

first floor of this house would be a comparatively simple matter, as so many pieces are built in. The handling of the woodwork and the various details of the construction could also be made an effective and important factor in the decoration of the rooms, and by a thoughtful study of the general arrangement a comfortable and homelike effect could be obtained.

Upstairs there are three bedrooms of convenient size and amply lighted, leading out of the small hall. The front bedroom opens upon the sleeping balcony at the side. Next to this room and just above the entry is a small sewing room provided with a convenient dresser.

LOW CRAFTSMAN ROCKER AND DROP-LEAF SEWING TABLE WHICH COULD BE USED IN THE LITTLE SEWING ROOM IN HOUSE NO. 85.

45

CRAFTSMAN CEMENT HOUSE, SIMPLE, COMFORTABLE AND SPACIOUS

Published in The Craftsman, July, 1910.

CRAFTSMAN CEMENT HOUSE, CONVENIENTLY PLANNED, WITH NINE ROOMS AND RECESSED DINING PORCH: NO. 94.

46

INTERIOR OF CEMENT HOUSE NO. 94, SHOWING DINING-ROOM SIDEBOARD AND CASEMENT WINDOWS ABOVE. THE SIMPLE TREATMENT OF THE HIGH WAINSCOTED WALL FORMS AN EXCELLENT BACKGROUND FOR THIS INTERESTING PIECE OF CRAFTSMAN FURNITURE.

THE walls of this house are of cement on metal lath and the roof is of red Ruberoid. The small roof over the entrance porch is of cement on metal lath like the walls, but the rafters that support it are of wood, and it rests upon heavy wooden beams. A variation in the color is given by the use of split field stone for the chimneys, one of which is revealed for its whole length, breaking the broad space at the end of the house. The severity of the wall in front is relieved by the spacing and grouping of the windows, and also by the recessed dining porch with its low parapet and row of

blooming plants that are placed along the top.

The entrance door is entirely of glass and with the windows on either side lights the front of the living room. Another group appears at the back, and the whole side wall is occupied by casements set high over bookshelves on either side of the central fireplace.

The division between living room and dining room is marked by the closets at either end. Casement windows are set high above the sideboard in the dining room, and in the wall at right angles to it. A glass door opens into the garden, and double glass doors with windows lead to the dining porch in front, which, being so effectually sheltered from the

DETAIL OF HAMMERED COPPER CHAFING DISH SHOWN IN INTERIOR VIEW OF HOUSE NO. 94.

DETAIL OF CIDER SET OF MARBLE-HEAD POTTERY AND COPPER TRAY SHOWN IN INTERIOR VIEW ABOVE.

THESE PIECES ARE ESPECIALLY SUITABLE, IN WORKMANSHIP, MATERIAL AND DESIGN, FOR CRAFTSMAN HOME.

CEMENT HOUSE WITH NINE ROOMS AND DINING PORCH

weather, could be used as an outdoor living room during a great part of the year. In winter it could be readily glassed in if desired, and would thus form an appreciable addition to the livable space within the house.

Perhaps one of the most interesting features ful craftsmanship and pleasing color and form.

The kitchen and servant's bedroom are placed in the one-story addition, so that they are entirely separated from the general plan of the house. The kitchen facilities are most conveniently contrived, and a storeroom and lavatory take up the space on either side of the hall that leads to the servant's bedroom. This arrangement is especially desirable, for the reason that it gives the maid her own quarters where she

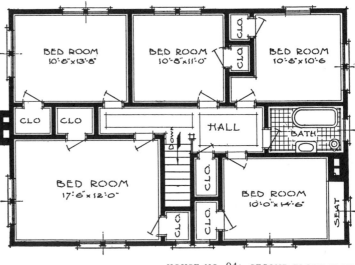

NO. 94:   CEMENT HOUSE: FIRST FLOOR PLAN.

of this construction is the simple but effective handling of the woodwork and wall spaces. As shown in the view of the dining room on the preceding page, the walls are wainscoted to the height of the frieze with V-jointed boards, finished in Craftsman style. This adds to the restfulness and unity of the interior, and forms a quiet and appropriate background for the furnishings, hangings and various details in the rooms. The treatment of the woodwork as shown here is especially in keeping with Craftsman furniture, and it will be noticed how the lines of the sideboard shown in the illustration carry out those of the general structural scheme. This piece of furniture, in fact, gives one a good idea of the satisfying effect that can be obtained by the thoughtful working out of a sturdy, practical and well-balanced design; and the larger details of the chafing dish and the set of pottery suggest, by their simple proportions, how much can be added to the beauty of a room by the choice of things which combine utility with care-

can come and go as she pleases without disturbing the rest of the house.

The second story has five bedrooms and a bath, grouped about a small central hall. The bathroom is floored with red cement marked off into squares, a plan that we usually follow in the Craftsman houses because it is attractive as well as sanitary and is very easy to keep clean.

HOUSE NO. 94: SECOND FLOOR PLAN.

SMALL BUT ROOMY ONE-STORY CEMENT BUNGA-LOW PLANNED FOR SIMPLIFIED HOUSEKEEPING

Published in The Craftsman, May, 1910.

ONE-STORY CEMENT BUNGALOW: NO. 90.

THIS one-story bungalow is meant for a small family, as it has room for only two bedrooms, but the arrangement of the interior is so compact that the maximum of room is afforded within the space enclosed by the outer walls. These are of cement on metal lath, with a roof of rough red slate and ridges of tile. The low, broad, sturdy effect is heightened by the use of buttresses which support the wide-eaved roof and give strength and dignity to the lines of the wall. The house has ample window space. Two small recessed porches at one end serve respectively as entrance porch and outdoor dining room. A glass door leads from the entrance porch directly into the living room.

The whole front of this room is taken up with the central group of windows and the casements set high on either side. A window seat is built below the middle group and bookcases occupy the remainder of the wall space to the height of the casements, and open shelves are built in on either side of the fireplace. The dining room, as is nearly always the case in a Craftsman house, is really a recess in the living room. A sideboard occupies the whole of the outside wall, with three casement windows set high above it. A glass door leads to the front porch, and the whole of the rear wall is taken up by casement windows and another glass

DETAIL OF CRAFTSMAN RECLINING CHAIR WITH AD-JUSTABLE BACK AND SPRING CUSHION SEAT, SHOWN ON THE NEXT PAGE IN INTERIOR VIEW OF BUNGALOW.

49

SMALL BUNGALOW PLANNED FOR SIMPLE HOUSEKEEPING

CORNER OF LIVING ROOM IN ONE-STORY BUNGALOW NO. 90, SHOWING OPEN SHELVES ON EACH SIDE OF THE FIREPLACE, AND EFFECTIVE USE OF CRAFTSMAN FURNISHINGS.

door leading to the rear porch. The room is thus well lighted and cheerful.

A tiny hall opening from the other end of the living room gives access to the two bedrooms and also to the kitchen, which by this means is entirely shut off from the remainder of the house. The bath is so placed that it is accessible from both bedrooms and from the kitchen.

The arrangement of this cottage is such that the house-mistress is practically independent of servants, for the compactness of the floor plan, the directness of the communication between the several rooms, and the convenient placing of the tables, closets, dressers, etc., in the kitchen and pantry, all help to minimize the necessary household work.

Another important factor is the presence of the several built-in pieces — sideboard, seat and bookshelves. These not only reduce the amount of furniture needed for the living room and dining room, but add considerably to their comfort and charm.

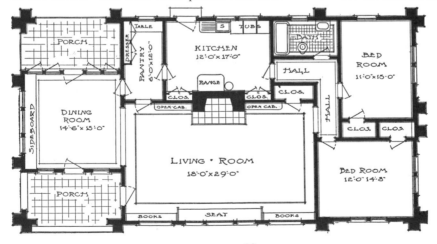

FLOOR PLAN OF ONE-STORY BUNGALOW: NO. 90.

CONCRETE COTTAGE WITH COMFORTABLE INTERIOR, DESIGNED TO ADMIT AMPLE LIGHT

Published in The Craftsman, February, 1907.   SEVEN-ROOM CONCRETE COTTAGE WITH THREE PORCHES: NO. 47.

IN designing this cottage we had in mind concrete or hollow cement block construction. Therefore the form of it is especially adapted to the use of such material, although the general plan admits of the use of brick or stone.

As we have shown it here, the side walls are broken into panels by raised bands of concrete which bind the corners and also run around the entire structure at the connection of the roof and between the first and second stories. These bands are smooth-surfaced, but the walls are made very rough by the simple process of washing off the surface with a brush and plenty of water immediately after the form is removed and while the material is set but still friable. If this is done at exactly the right time, the washing-brush can be so applied as to remove the mortar to a considerable depth between the aggregates, leaving them in relief and producing a rough texture that is very interesting.

The plan of this house is not unlike a Greek cross, the rooms being

so arranged that the greatest possible space is available and also an unusual amount of light and air. The foundation is of concrete and is continued upward on a gentle slant from

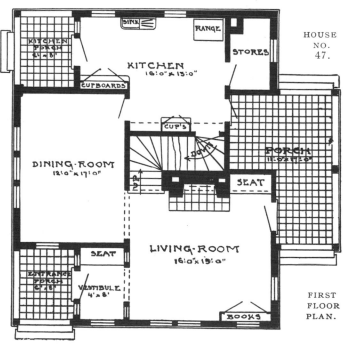

51

CONCRETE COTTAGE WITH SEVEN ROOMS AND THREE PORCHES

INTERIOR VIEW OF CONCRETE COTTAGE NO. 47, SHOWING A CORNER OF THE LIVING ROOM, AND GLIMPSES OF THE VESTIBULE, DINING ROOM AND STAIRCASE. THE BUILT-IN SEATS AND DECORATIVE HANDLING OF THE WOODWORK ARE ESPECIALLY INTERESTING.

the ground to a line at the base of the windows on the first floor, which gives a continuous horizontal line on a level with the parapets of the corner porches.

The rear porch is recessed and extends the whole width of the wing, being large enough to serve as a very comfortable outdoor dining room. For this style of house we would recommend that all the porches be floored with red cement divided into squares.

The interior of the cottage is somewhat unique in plan, and the arrangement of the rooms is unusually convenient. The built-in seat in the vestibule and beside the living room hearth, the built-in bookshelves above the latter seat, and those in the opposite corner of the room, add to the comfort as well as the homelike appearance of the whole, and the way in which the woodwork is handled is distinctly decorative and will prove a helpful factor in the task of furnishing. The paneled wainscot, the spindles above the openings between the living room and the dining room and vestibule, and the pleasant handling of wall spaces can be seen in the sketch of the interior on this page. The various details, of course, would be worked out to suit the taste and convenience of the owner, and the illustration and floor plan may serve to suggest many delightful possibilities of decoration.

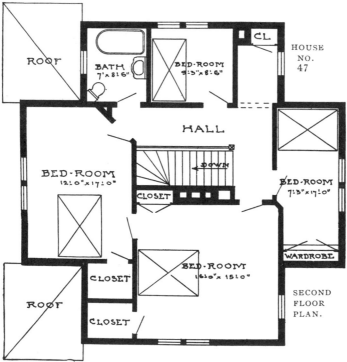

HOUSE NO. 47

SECOND FLOOR PLAN.

52

INEXPENSIVE CEMENT CONSTRUCTION FOR SUMMER AND WEEK-END ONE-STORY BUNGALOW

ALTHOUGH so simple in construction that the owner can assist in building it, this little bungalow will prove a well-planned, serviceable and attractive dwelling. The walls sunshine to each one of the five rooms within.

In spite of the extreme simplicity of its construction and lay-out of the interior—or perhaps we should rather say because of this

Published in The Craftsman, December, 1909.

INEXPENSIVE CEMENT BUNGALOW: NO. 80.

and partitions are of cement mortar upon metal lath. The girders of the house are supported upon concrete piers, less expensive than a stone foundation. The base of the chimney runs to the depth of the piers. The porch floor may be of cinder concrete, the same as used for sidewalks, slightly slanted so that it will drain easily, and the porch roof supports are of logs. The rafters are sheathed with V-jointed boards, dressed, and finished on the under side. These boards make the only ceiling to the cottage, and above them are laid strips of Ruberoid roofing. Within, all the structural beams are left exposed and are smoothed and stained.

The big chimney in the living room contains also the flue of the kitchen range. Besides these two rooms there are two bedrooms, a bathroom and many convenient closets, the arrangement, as the floor plan shows, being both compact and convenient.

The groups of windows with their small square panes not only add a touch of interest to the plain cement walls of the building, but give ample air and simplicity—the bungalow, when comfortably and tastefully furnished, should make a very charming little summer home, and would certainly permit a minimizing of all housework

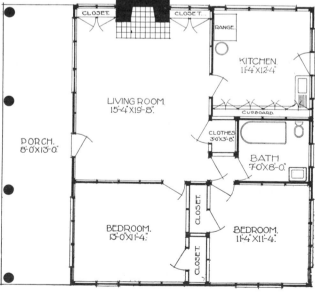

FLOOR PLAN OF CEMENT BUNGALOW: NO. 80.

TWO-STORY CEMENT BUNGALOW WITH AMPLE PORCH ROOM AND COMFORTABLE INTERIOR

Published in The Craftsman, December, 1909.

TWO-STORY CEMENT BUNGALOW WITH FIVE ROOMS AND PORCH: NO. 81.

WHILE this cottage is more elaborate in design than the one-story bungalow shown on the preceding page, the same general construction is used, cement mortar upon metal lath being chosen for the walls, stone for the chimney, logs for the pillars of the porch and cinder concrete for the porch floor. In this cottage, however, the roof is shingled. The exterior, though quite unpretentious, is pleasing in line and proportion, with its well-placed windows, sloping dormer and sheltered angle of the long, roomy porch.

The illustration of the living room will also furnish an idea of the appearance of the living room of the previous bungalow, inasmuch as the main structural beams are the same. Indeed, all the woodwork in the living room, with the exception of the baseboard, which is cut in between the studs, is simply the necessary structural beams. The stairs lead up from the right, and a curtain may be hung to shield those about the hearth from any draught that may come from the upper rooms.

A door from one corner of the living room

VIEW OF STONE FIREPLACE IN LIVING ROOM OF TWO-STORY BUNGALOW, NO. 81. THE WOODWORK SHOWN IN THIS INTERIOR IS SIMPLY THE STRUCTURAL BEAMS OF THE BUILDING.

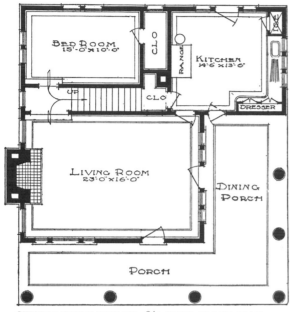

CEMENT BUNGALOW NO. 81: FIRST FLOOR PLAN.

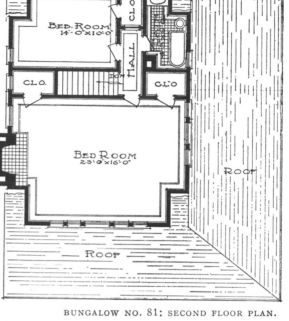

BUNGALOW NO. 81: SECOND FLOOR PLAN.

leads into the kitchen, which is large, well lighted and conveniently arranged. On the first floor there is also a bedroom provided with a large closet. The smaller closet beside it opens into the kitchen.

On the upper floor are two bedrooms and a bath, leading out of a small hall. The front bedroom is a large, cheerful apartment, with plenty of windows, and provided with an open fireplace which uses the same chimney as the one in the living room just below. Two good-sized closets are placed at opposite corners. Both this bedroom and the one in the rear could be made charming and comfortable by the use of window or corner seats and simple furnishings.

The arrangements of the rooms on each floor are so simple and compact that it would be an easy matter to

keep them in order, and the accommodation would be quite sufficient for a small family.

Both this bungalow and the one previously described are intended exclusively for summer use. Either of them, however, could be built with an inside wall which would fit them also for winter, but this, of course, would add greatly to the expense. One of the chief advantages of both constructions shown is that when closed for the winter there is no place in which mice would build their nests or mildew collect. Every part of the cottage is open to the air. Returning in the spring, the owner needs only to brush down the cobwebs and wipe away the dust to find himself settled and at home for the summer.

CANDLESTICK, ANDIRONS AND BOWL FOR A CRAFTSMAN INTERIOR.

THESE FITTINGS ARE SO SIMPLE AND ARTISTIC THAT THEY WILL HARMONIZE WITH ANY FURNISHINGS.

TWO-STORY HOUSE FOR VILLAGE CORNER PLOT

A VILLAGE corner plot of average size (60 x 150) is the site for which the house was designed, keeping in mind the usual restrictions which limit the building line to within forty feet of the front street, fifteen feet of the side street, and five feet of the side line. The walls are covered with cement stucco and the roof is of slate. The chimney is carried up full size, and being in the center of the house, forms an apex for the four corners of the roof. The two balconies and the various groups of windows, the broad veranda

tween them opening onto the dining porch at the back of the house. From the dining room, swing doors lead through the large pantry, with its ice-box and ample shelves, into the kitchen, which communicates in turn with the laundry at the rear.

A small square den is provided off one side of the living room, and next to this the staircase goes up to the landing and thence to the second floor. This staircase, as the interior view indicates, forms an interesting part of the living room, and the Craftsman newel-post

Published in The Craftsman, April, 1911.   CEMENT HOUSE WITH NINE ROOMS AND DINING PORCH: NO. 113.

with its cement floor, and the end flower-boxes which serve at the same time as screens, are all pleasant exterior features.

In the lay-out of the rooms we have considered the particular requirements of a family living in the suburbs. The entrance is through a vestibule in which is the coat closet. The living room is a large cheerful apartment, lighted by groups of windows on two sides, and provided with an open fireplace. A wide opening leads into the dining room beyond, through which a pleasant vista is given by the windows at the end and glass door be-

lamp is a useful as well as a decorative feature. This house may be heated with a Craftsman fireplace-furnace, the living room, dining room and two rear bedrooms being heated by warm air, and the other rooms having hot-water heat, both supplied from the fireplace-furnace.

We have located the laundry on the first floor, as it will serve as a summer kitchen during the hot days, and also is a suitable place for preparing vegetables, canning fruit, etc. The rear porch may be screened for use as an open-air dining room in the summer, and the screens can be replaced with sash to provide

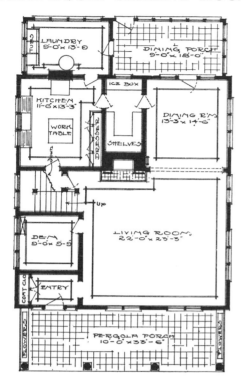

HOUSE NO. 113: FIRST FLOOR PLAN.

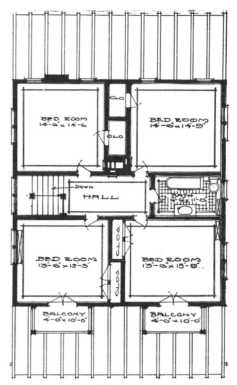

HOUSE NO. 113: SECOND FLOOR PLAN.

a cheerful sun room during winter months.

The upper rooms are very simply arranged, with a square bedroom at each corner of the floor plan, opening out of the central hall. Each bedroom is lighted with windows on two sides, and is provided with a closet. The two front rooms are especially pleasant, as each has double glass doors giving access to a small balcony placed over the roof of the pergola porch.

GLIMPSE OF LIVING ROOM IN CEMENT HOUSE, NO. 113, SHOWING TILED CHIMNEYPIECE AND DECORATIVE TREATMENT OF DOORS, WOODWORK AND WALL SPACES.

MODERATE-SIZED CRAFTSMAN HOUSE COMBINING BOTH PRIVACY AND HOSPITALITY

Published in The Craftsman, April, 1911.

NINE-ROOM CEMENT HOUSE WITH PORCHES
AND SLEEPING BALCONIES: NO. 114.

THIS house is planned for a middle lot on a village street. Cement stucco is used for the walls of the building, and the roof is of slate. The recessed porches in the front and the large sleeping balcony in the rear are interesting exterior features. The floor plans are worked out with the idea of economy in space, and yet nothing has been sacrificed in comfort or convenience.

The living room and dining room are separated by the entry; no vestibule has been provided, as the entrance door is well protected by the recessed porch. The coat closet and stairs are located in the entry, and the fireplace is screened by bookshelves built in between the supporting posts of the overhead beams.

The large living room has a direct opening on the rear veranda, and on either side of this is a long built-in bookcase with a group of three win-

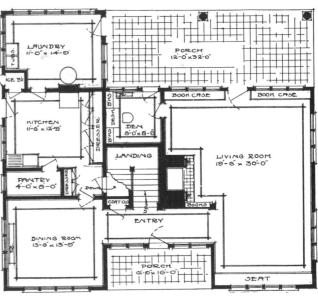

HOUSE NO. 114: FIRST FLOOR PLAN

dows set in the wall above, overlooking the porch. There are two more window groups in the side wall, and another in the recess at the front, where a long window seat is built in. The irregular shape of the room, with its various nooks and corners, and the interest derived from the careful handling of the necessary structural features, combine to make an unusually charming interior. The sketch shown here of the fireplace corner gives one some impression of the general effect, and suggests many delightful possibilities in the way of furnishing. In fact, with a few simple pieces, chosen for comfort and beauty, with a carefully worked-out color scheme, and the addition of those little individual touches in furnishing and decoration which must always be left to the personal taste of the owner, the apartment could be made very homelike and hospitable.

The small den communicates directly with the living room and rear veranda, and here too the built-in bookcases and a desk add to the comfort. Ample closet and pantry room are provided in the kitchen, and a built-in ice-box is planned with outside door for putting in ice. The open laundry may be screened in summer and glazed in winter, and serves also as a summer kitchen. If a Craftsman fire-

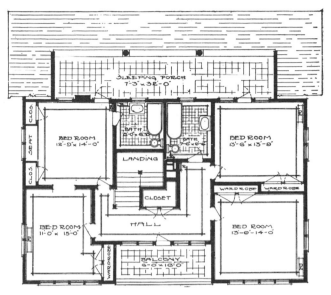

HOUSE NO. 114: SECOND FLOOR PLAN.

place-furnace is used, as shown here, the cellar may be omitted.

The recessed balcony under the roof is a delightful addition to the upper rooms. Two of the bedrooms are arranged so that they may be used *en suite* with private bath.

CORNER OF LIVING ROOM IN CRAFTSMAN HOUSE NO. 114: THE USE OF TILES FOR THE FIREPLACE-FURNACE, THE PLACING OF THE BOOKSHELVES AND THE LONG WINDOW SEAT, AND THE GLIMPSE OF THE WELL-LIGHTED ENTRY, SUGGEST AN UNUSUALLY INTERESTING INTERIOR.

CRAFTSMAN HOUSE DESIGNED FOR CITY OR SUBURBAN LOT

Published in The Craftsman, June, 1911.   COMPACTLY PLANNED, EIGHT-ROOM CEMENT HOUSE: NO. 117.

CEMENT stucco on metal lath is used for this house, which is intended for a city or suburban lot. The wide pergola and balcony, the stone and brick chimneys and groups of casements present a homelike and pleasing appearance. Purposely we have set the house down so as to show only a suggestion of the foundation. Instead of having a cellar, we prefer to level up the space between the walls of the foundation with earth, topping this with cinders and cinder concrete to a level of the foundation walls, and using 2 x 4's embedded in this for the first floor beams.

The interior has been arranged to eliminate all unnecessary partitions, and the stairs lead up directly from the living room. A den or workroom has been provided off the living room. Seats are built in beside each fireplace, and the one in the dining room has been so placed as to serve in connection with the table. Placing the table in this position allows ample space around the fireplace and does not give an appearance of being crowded, so often the

case when fireplaces are built in the dining room. The house may be heated and ventilated by using Craftsman fireplace-furnaces.

The view of the fireplace end of the living room, with its corner seat, built-in bookshelves, and casement windows above, gives some idea of the general effect of the interior. The treatment of woodwork and wall spaces is simple but effective, and serves as a restful background for the various furnishings. The tiled hearth, the decorative placing of the bricks in the chimneypiece, and the recess above the shelf, add to the attraction of the inglenook, which, with its comfortable seats and inviting books, naturally becomes the center of interest of the room. The walls could be left plain or could be stenciled as suggested in the illustration with some design that would help to carry out the general color scheme of the interior. The woodwork of the staircase in the opposite corner of the living room could also be handled in such a way as to give structural beauty to this necessary feature.

COMPACTLY PLANNED, EIGHT-ROOM CEMENT HOUSE

CORNER OF LIVING ROOM IN CRAFTSMAN CEMENT HOUSE NO. 117, SHOWING THE FIREPLACE-FURNACE AND BUILT-IN SEAT AND BOOKSHELVES IN THE INGLENOOK.

The second floor is quite simple in arrangement, a bedroom occupying each of the four corners of the plan, with the bathroom between the smaller bedrooms on one side. Three of the bedrooms open into the hall, which is wide and cheerful and terminates a few steps down on the stair landing at the rear. From this landing several steps lead up to the other back chamber. All four of the bedrooms have windows on two sides, and ample closet room is provided.

Perhaps one of the most attractive features of this upper floor plan is the little balcony in the front over the pergola porch. Part of this balcony is open, protected by a railing, and part is recessed, as shown.

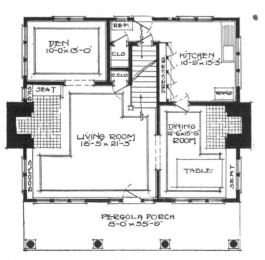

CEMENT HOUSE NO. 117: FIRST FLOOR PLAN.

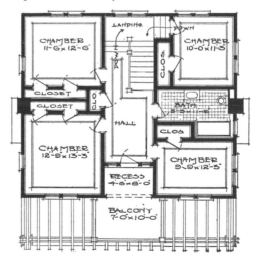

HOUSE NO. 117: SECOND FLOOR PLAN.

61

CEMENT COTTAGE FOR A NARROW TOWN LOT

Published in The Craftsman, June, 1911.

CRAFTSMAN CEMENT COTTAGE NO. 118.

THIS cement cottage is planned for a narrow lot and is only a story and a half high. It has a long roof line broken with flat dormers front and rear. The groups of windows are most interesting, all being casement except the large plate glass picture window of the front group, which is stationary. No front veranda has been provided; but the entry is recessed and the graceful arch emphasizes the cement construction. Hollyhocks would be especially charming against the plain walls.

On entering, you find the hall space has been included in the living room, with an open stair conveniently located near the entrance. A partition dividing dining and living room is only suggested—an arrangement which permits of a vista from living room through dining room and across the rear porch. Open bookshelves break up the long wall of the living room and a space has been left for the piano, which will give it an appearance of being built in.

The Craftsman fireplace-furnace is large and generous, and with the inviting seat nearby becomes at once the center of interest. The

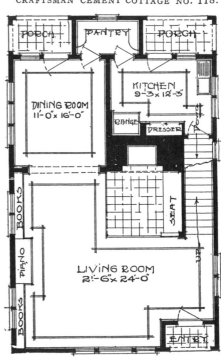

HOUSE NO. 118: FIRST FLOOR PLAN.

CEMENT COTTAGE FOR A NARROW TOWN LOT

CRAFTSMAN LANTERN WHICH COULD BE USED IN THE INTERIOR SHOWN BELOW.

fireplace is built of common brick and is plastered, while color may be introduced by the use of tile porcelain for the inside panel on which the hammered copper hood is placed.

The view which is given below of one corner of the living room, with its fireplace, fireside seat and glimpse of the stairway behind, suggests an interesting method of handling the woodwork, and gives a general impression of the treatment of the various structural features of the interior. As is usual in a Craftsman house, these possess decorative quality without being in the least elaborate, and while they add to the beauty of the rooms they also help to minimize the task of furnishing.

The kitchen, which is a convenient size, communicates with the dining room through the pantry, which is built out between the two corner porches at the rear. A door from the kitchen also opens upon the adjacent porch.

The second floor is conveniently arranged with three bedrooms, ample closets and a large storeroom, the closets being built under the roof and not being full height except at the front. The storeroom and the large closets

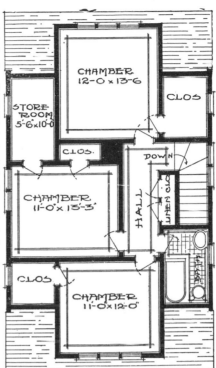

CRAFTSMAN CEMENT COTTAGE: SECOND FLOOR PLAN.

against the outer walls are lighted by small windows. The staircase is also well lighted.

ONE CORNER OF THE LIVING ROOM IN CEMENT COTTAGE NO. 118, SHOWING ARRANGEMENT OF THE CRAFTSMAN FIREPLACE-FURNACE, WITH BUILT-IN SEAT AND STAIRWAY BEHIND IT.

INEXPENSIVE AND HOMELIKE COTTAGE OF STONE AND SHINGLE, FOR SIMPLE HOUSEKEEPING

IN the cottage shown here, split stone is used for the walls and for the parapet and pillars of the front porch. The steps and floor of this porch are of cement. The gables are shingled with split cypress shingles, and the roof is also shingled, with the rafters left exposed at the widely overhanging eaves.

The interior of this cottage is very compactly and conveniently arranged, the idea being to make it easy for the mistress of the house to do her own work if she so desires. At one end there are two bedrooms and a good-sized bathroom, shut off from the rest of the house by a small hall that affords access to five rooms—the dining room and kitchen as well as the bedrooms and the bath. It also separates the kitchen from the dining room, so that all odors of cooking are shut off from the front part of the house. The dining room is placed directly in front with the two high windows above the sideboard looking out upon the front porch. The room itself is small, but there is no feeling of being cramped for space because the wide opening into the sitting room makes it to all intents and purposes a recess in the larger room. The sitting room, with the large fireside nook at the back, occupies the whole end of the house. Like the sitting room, this nook is wainscoted with chestnut to the height of the broad beam that marks the angle of the ceiling, so that the whole wall is of wood. The large chimneypiece of split field stone extends to the ceiling, and the recesses on either side are filled with bookshelves. Seats are built in on each side of the nook, the panels at the ends serving the double purpose of suggesting a separation from the main room and furnishing the seat ends. The ceilings are tinted to a tone that harmonizes with the soft greenish brown of the chestnut.

Published in The Craftsman, July, 1910.

INEXPENSIVE COTTAGE OF STONE AND SHINGLE, PLANNED FOR SIMPLE HOUSEKEEPING: NO. 93.

INEXPENSIVE CRAFTSMAN COTTAGE OF STONE AND SHINGLE

INGLENOOK IN SITTING ROOM OF CRAFTSMAN COTTAGE, NO. 93, SHOWING STONE CHIMNEYPIECE WITH BUILT-IN BOOKSHELVES AND SEAT ON EITHER SIDE, AND GLIMPSE OF STAIRWAY WITH NEWEL-POST LAMP AT THE RIGHT.

In the view of this inglenook a glimpse of the staircase to the right is also seen. This forms an interesting part of the structural woodwork of the interior, and if the newel post is fitted with a lamp as suggested in the illustration a very decorative effect is obtained.

In the front bedroom which opens out upon the porch, there is a built-in seat beneath the window, occupying the recess formed by the small corner closets on either hand. The cottage, on the whole, is one which would require very little movable furniture to make it ready for its occupants, and in addition to the economical advantage of the built-in pieces, they add to the unity of the interior by the way in which they carry out the general effect of the rest of the woodwork,—wainscot, beams, etc.

—giving the rooms an air of permanency and repose that is very homelike.

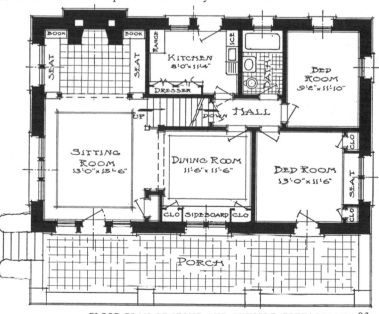

FLOOR PLAN OF STONE AND SHINGLE COTTAGE: NO. 93.

65

STONE AND SHINGLE HOUSE, WITH SEVEN ROOMS AND RECESSED ENTRANCE PORCH

Published in The Craftsman, December, 1911.

SEVEN-ROOM STONE AND SHINGLE HOUSE: NO. 126.

THE foundation, chimneys and lower walls of this house are of split stone; above this, hand-split cypress shingles are used for the walls and sawed red cedar shingles for the roof.

One of the most attractive features of the exterior is the recessed entrance porch, better

shown in the enlarged detail view on the next page. The simple lines of the stonework, the low curve of the arch, broken by the graceful touch of vines, the wide Dutch door with small square lights set in the upper half, the window and bracket lantern on each side, and the bench beneath the dining-room window,—

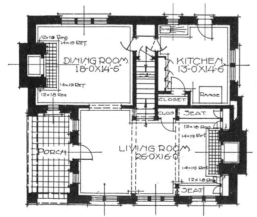

CRAFTSMAN HOUSE NO. 126: FIRST FLOOR PLAN.

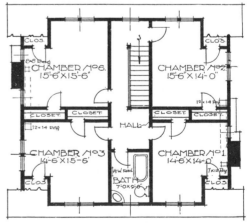

HOUSE NO. 126: SECOND FLOOR PLAN.

66

SEVEN-ROOM HOUSE WITH RECESSED PORCH

DETAIL VIEW OF
RECESSED PORCH
HOUSE NO. 126

all combine to make the approach to the house especially inviting, indicating at the same time by the simple sincerity of treatment, the prevailing characteristic of the home within.

One enters from the porch directly into the living room, which is large, light and hospitable, and the interest centers at once in the pleasant inglenook at the farther end. Tapestry brick is used for the chimneypiece of the Craftsman fireplace-furnace, which, with the one in the dining room, serves to heat and ventilate the whole building. Front and rear dormers give ample height to the four bedrooms and bath on the second story.

CORNER OF INGLENOOK IN LIVING ROOM OF HOUSE NO. 126, SHOWING FIREPLACE-FURNACE, BOOKSHELVES AND SEAT.

ROOMY CRAFTSMAN HOUSE IN WHICH STONE, CEMENT AND WOOD ARE USED

Published in The Craftsman, August, 1909.

TWO-STORY CRAFTSMAN HOUSE: NO. 72.

STONE, cement and wood are used in the construction of this two-story house, the foundation and lower walls being of stone and the upper walls shingled. The roof is broken into a dormer, and is covered, like the porch, with a composition roofing. The rafters and purlins are left exposed. The base of the chimney is of split field stone like the parapet, but brick is used toward the upper part, as shown.

The windows of the second story are hooded and are both casement and the double-hung variety. The double-hung window has a single pane of glass in the lower sash, and six small panes in the upper sash. This contrast makes a very attractive effect seen from the outside, and also obviates looking out through small panes, which some people dislike. Throughout the lower story window groups are used, consisting of a double-hung window made in the fashion of those on the second story, with a single casement set on either side.

The detail view of the exterior on the opposite page shows the pergola at one end of the porch, and the bay window of the dining room. The roof of the pergola, as well as that of the porch, is supported upon a wood beam resting upon pillars of cement. These pillars stand upon the stone posts of the parapet, between which run cement flower-boxes. The steps and parapet are of split field stone.

The side entrance under the pergola leads into a big open hall between the dining room and living room; the front entrance opens into a vestibule leading into another open hallway between the living room and den. At the rear of this is a landing raised about two steps, and from this landing the stairs go up to the second story. A railing separates the landing from the big side hall and makes a very interesting background to the room as one enters from the pergola. The lower story is very open, with the exception of the kitchen which is sufficiently separated to prevent any odor of cooking penetrating the rest of the house. It is well fitted with shelves and closets, and connects with the dining room through a butler's pantry. At the end of another closet two steps lead up to the landing so that the maid has a direct passage from the kitchen to the door. The upstairs plan explains itself. A flight of stairs leads to the attic where two rooms may be finished for use if desired.

ROOMY TWO-STORY CRAFTSMAN HOUSE

HOUSE NO. 72: DETAIL OF PERGOLA PORCH SHOWING INTERESTING VARIETY OF BUILDING MATERIALS.

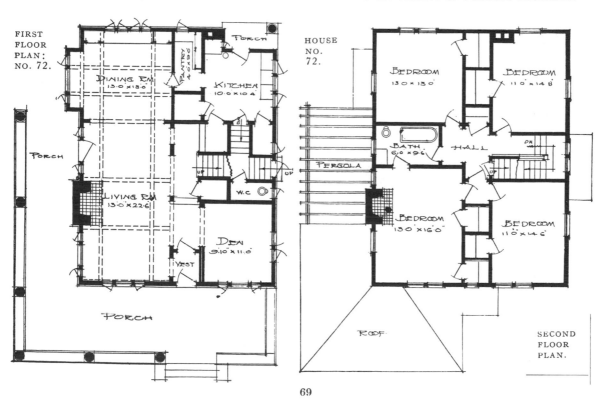

FIRST FLOOR PLAN: NO. 72.

PORCH

DINING RM 13·0"×13·0"

PANTRY 4·0"×9·0"

KITCHEN 10·0"×10·4"

PORCH

W.C

LIVING RM 13·0"×22·6"

DEN 9·10"×11·0"

VEST

PORCH

HOUSE NO. 72.

BEDROOM 13·0"×13·0"

BEDROOM 11·0"×14·8"

BATH 6·0"×9·6"

HALL

PERGOLA

BEDROOM 13·0"×16·0"

BEDROOM 11·0"×14·6"

ROOF

SECOND FLOOR PLAN.

CRAFTSMAN STONE HOUSE WITH PRACTICAL BUILT-IN FITTINGS

Published in The Craftsman, July, 1909.

REAR VIEW OF STONE HOUSE, NO. 71.

ALTHOUGH we have shown this house of stone, with heavy timber lintels and composition roofing, the design could be worked out in other materials. Glass doors open from dining room and living room upon a terrace with parapet and posts of stone, cement floor and flower-boxes. The railing of the sleeping balcony above is supported upon the exposed timbers of the house. This and the two casements on either side form practically a dormer construction.

The house is entered from the front through a hallway with doors leading to the living room, dining room and kitchen. On each side of the

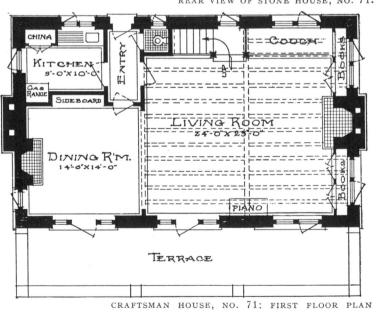

CRAFTSMAN HOUSE, NO. 71: FIRST FLOOR PLAN

STONE HOUSE WITH PRACTICAL BUILT-IN FITTINGS

living-room fireplace, with its hood of hammered copper, are built-in bookcases with convenient drawers below and windows above. The dining room is separated from the living room only by a shallow grille running along the ceiling, and the sideboard is built into the room. The kitchen is connected with the dining room by the entry.

On the second floor the small hall gives access to the bathroom, two large bedrooms and a smaller one between. The bedroom at the right has a big open fireplace which uses the same chimney as that in the living room below, and on either side of this are casement windows. In each corner of the room is a closet, and beneath the windows in the recess formed by the closets is a built-in seat. In the bedroom on the opposite side of the house there is a somewhat smaller fireplace and a similar arrangement of corner closets and recessed window seat in front. Each of the bedrooms has a door opening out onto the sleeping balcony.

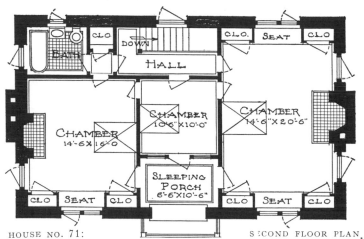

HOUSE NO. 71: SECOND FLOOR PLAN.

As the drawings and description indicate, the interior is one which could be very easily furnished, for there are already so many built-in pieces that the rooms seem hospitably ready to be occupied even before the owner has moved in his personal possessions. The simple but effective treatment of the woodwork and the interest derived from the frank handling of the many structural features are full of suggestions for the arranging of the more intimate details in the furnishing of a home.

INTERIOR OF HOUSE NO. 71: CORNER OF LIVING ROOM WITH FIREPLACE AND BUILT-IN FITTINGS.

ROUGH STONE HOUSE COMBINING COMFORT AND PICTURESQUENESS

Published in The Craftsman, June, 1909.
STONE HOUSE WITH SEVEN ROOMS, BREAKFAST PORCH AND RECESSED SLEEPING BALCONY: NO. 69.

STONE HOUSE COMBINING COMFORT AND PICTURESQUENESS

ROUGH stone is the material used for this house. The timbers are left exposed, making a rugged finish consistent with the stone exterior. The dormers, gracefully proportioned and in harmonious relation to the slope of the roof, are fitted with simple casements opening upon garden boxes. In the windows of the lower story, the middle section is a stationary panel of glass, and the two outside sections are outward-opening casements. On the sides of the house are smaller windows, similar in shape, which have a double casement in place of the glass panel.

The interior view on page 74 shows a rear corner of the living room. The chimneypiece suggests

HOUSE NO. 69:
SECOND FLOOR
PLAN.

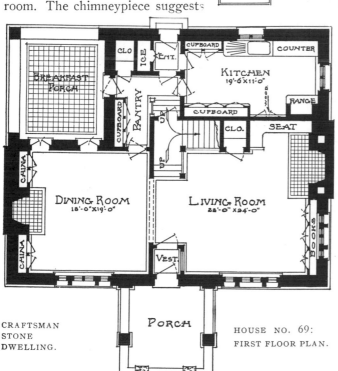

CRAFTSMAN
STONE
DWELLING.

HOUSE NO. 69:
FIRST FLOOR PLAN.

piece are built-in bookcases with casement windows above. There is a convenient closet between the fireside seat and the staircase, and the latter is accessible from both living room and pantry. A wide opening leads into the dining room which is also provided with an open fireplace with built-in china closets on each side. Doors lead from the dining room to the corner breakfast porch at the rear, which can also be reached from the kitchen through the swinging doors of the pantry.

On the second floor there are three good-sized bedrooms, and a small sewing room, each of which is fitted with a comfortable built-in window seat in the recess formed by the dormer. Under the slope of the roof, in front and at the four corners of the house, closets are provided, and there are also closets between the interior walls. One end of the L-shaped hall leads onto a small recessed sleeping porch at the rear. This, being protected by walls on three sides, is sufficiently sheltered to be of use in practically all sorts of weather, and the front could be further screened with an awning if necessary.

the exterior of the house because it is of the same material, bringing the whole into closer relation. The seat in the wainscoted inglenook is as useful as it is attractive. By lifting up the top, one finds the logs for the hearth fire, placed there through a little door from the kitchen. On the other side of the chimney-

See Pages 72 and 73.
CORNER OF LIVING ROOM IN STONE HOUSE NO. 69, SHOWING ARRANGEMENT OF FIREPLACE, BUILT-IN CORNER SEAT AND BOOK-CASES WITH CASEMENT WINDOWS ABOVE.

EIGHT-ROOM BUNGALOW OF STONE AND CEMENT

Published in The Craftsman, April, 1909.

EIGHT-ROOM CRAFTSMAN BUNGALOW: NO. 65.

IN this bungalow, which is suitable for either country or suburbs, we have used split field stone for the walls of the lower story and for the square pillars of the porch. The gables are plastered, with half-timber construction, and the roof is shingled.

This kind of building lends itself admirably to the use of heavy timbers such as appear all around the walls at the top of the first story, and in keeping with this effect are the exposed rafters and girders which support the widely overhanging roof. Especially decorative is the construction over the recess in the middle of the porch, the beams being raised as shown in the illustration, admitting more light to the living room.

Just above is the sleeping porch, also recessed for a part of its depth, and protected by a heavy wooden balustrade. This porch affords ample room for two beds, and it would be easy to throw a partition across the center, dividing it into two outdoor sleeping rooms,—an arrangement made the more practicable by the two glass doors which lead to this

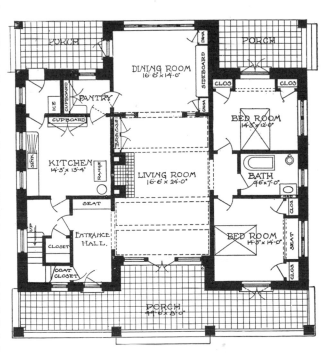

BUNGALOW NO. 65: FIRST FLOOR PLAN

porch from the upper hall.

The floor plan shows a typical Craftsman interior, the details of which could be adapted to the owner's needs. The door from the porch opens into an entrance hall with closets and staircase on one side and an inviting seat built into the wall directly opposite the front door. A wide opening on the right leads into the large living room with its open fireplace, built-in bookcase, and glass door opening onto the front porch. The dining room is in the rear running out between two corner porches, onto one of which it opens. There is a group of four windows at the back of the room, and built-in sideboard and china closets along one side. Between the dining room and living room post and panel construction is used, the wide opening accentuating the space of the lower story. Swinging doors through the pantry lead from the dining room into the kitchen, which is fitted with every convenience for housekeeping, and from which access can also be had to the adjacent corner porch. A door leads also from the kitchen to the lower stairway hall and entrance hall in front.

On the other side of the floor plan are two bedrooms and a bath, somewhat separated from the rest of the house by a small private hall. In both bedrooms there are two corner closets and in the front room there is also a built-in window seat. Each room has long double glass doors opening out onto the front and rear porches respectively.

On the second floor is another bedroom, also fitted with corner closets and built-in window seat. On the other side of the hall is the maid's room, and at the back a billiard room with long seats at each end and a group of

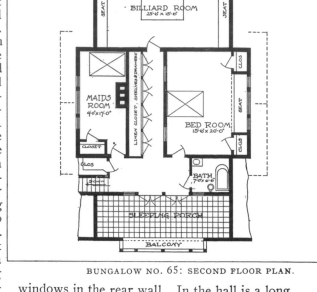

BUNGALOW NO. 65: SECOND FLOOR PLAN.

windows in the rear wall. In the hall is a long and very convenient linen closet with shelves and drawers. A small bathroom is also provided on this floor, and doors lead from the hall onto the sleeping balcony, as previously described.

The pieces from the Craftsman workshops shown on this page, being simple in design, sturdily made, and harmonizing with the woodwork of a Craftsman interior, suggest the style of furniture best adapted for these rooms.

CRAFTSMAN COTTAGE OF STONE, SHINGLE AND SLATE: A PRACTICAL AND COMFORTABLE HOME

Published in The Craftsman, March, 1911.

COTTAGE OF STONE, SHINGLE AND SLATE, WITH SEVEN ROOMS, DINING PORCH AND SLEEPING BALCONIES: NO. 111.

THE attractiveness of the design, the harmonious colors of the different building materials used, and the well-arranged floor plans combine to make this house especially interesting. The exterior is of stone, rived shingles and slate. The open construction of the roof, together with the rough texture of the stone, will be found sufficiently rustic to be in keeping with the surrounding hills and woods.

Care should be taken in selecting the building stone. Field stone, when split and laid up in irregular shapes and sizes, forms the most pleasing effect.

The entry and fireplace nook are wainscoted with V-jointed boards, but all other walls and ceilings are plastered. The broad surfaces are broken up in panels by extending the door and window casings from baseboard to frieze, and by the large beams on the ceiling.

The fireplace is laid up of split stone, the same as used for exterior walls, but in the selection of this more care has to be exercised. The hammered copper hood harmonizes with the variegated surfaces of the stone. The Craftsman fireplace-furnace is shown installed here, furnishing heat and ventilation for the entire house.

The living room is large and well lighted

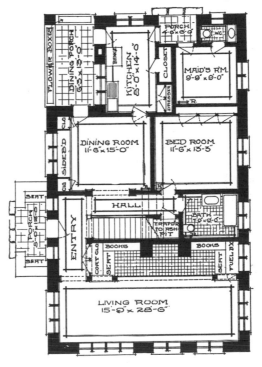

COTTAGE NO. 111: FIRST FLOOR PLAN.

with several groups of casement windows. The illustration below shows one corner of this room, with the stone fireplace, built-in bookshelves on either side, and wainscoted seats of the inglenook. The simple decorative treatment of the woodwork with its post and panel construction, the charm of the small-paned casement windows, and the glimpse of the entry on the right and the bottom of the staircase with its newel-post lamp, suggest something of the general appearance of the interior, and give one an idea of the homelike quality that results from this frank handling of the various structural features.

Built-in sideboard and china closets occupy the entire end of the dining room, and the open dining porch, slightly screened in with flowers, affords a delightful place for outdoor meals. The floor of this porch is of cement. The owner's bedroom and bath, as well as the room for the maid, are located on the first floor. The kitchen is large, well lighted and so arranged as to be easily accessible from the dining room, dining porch and maid's room, while not connecting directly with the latter. The little recessed kitchen porch serves also as a porch for the maid.

On the second floor only two bedrooms and a bath are provided. These rooms, although in the attic, are worked out with full-height ceilings, and by the aid of dormers cross-ventilation is provided which renders them as comfortable and livable as though the house were full two stories.

A charming feature of these bedrooms is the

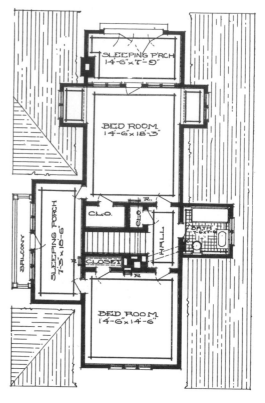

COTTAGE NO. 111: SECOND FLOOR PLAN

sleeping porches. While the end of each one is left open, provision has been made to shut out bad weather, and since they are built within the house they may be glassed in, making delightful sunrooms for winter days.

INTERIOR OF COTTAGE NO. 111, SHOWING LIVING-ROOM INGLENOOK WITH CRAFTSMAN FIREPLACE-FURNACE, BUILT-IN BOOKSHELVES AND SEATS. AT THE LEFT IS A GLIMPSE OF STAIRCASE FITTED WITH NEWEL-POST LAMP.

BRICK COTTAGE WITH CONVENIENT BUILT-IN FURNISHINGS AND AMPLE PORCH ROOM

Published in The Craftsman, March, 1911.

BRICK COTTAGE WITH SIX ROOMS, DINING PORCH AND PERGOLA: NO. 112.

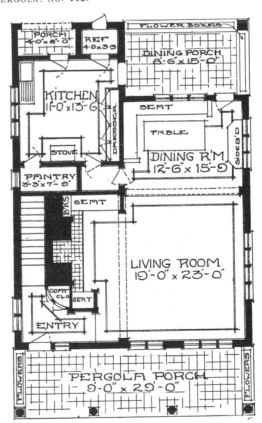

COTTAGE NO. 112: FIRST FLOOR PLAN.

BRICK on a stone foundation is used for this cottage. The common dark-colored, hard-burned brick (laid up in Dutch bond with half-inch joints) blends in texture and color with the rived shingles and rough slates of gables and roof. A section of the roof on either side is raised up, forming a flat dormer which accentuates the low bungalow effect. An interesting feature is found in the pergola porch, the ends being carried up about three feet and flower-boxes built into the walls.

The entry is provided with conveniently arranged coat closet, and is one step higher than the living room. The living room and the dining room are planned as one, the latter being merely an alcove raised a step above the living room proper. The fireplace nook is large and is shown provided with the Craftsman fireplace-furnace.

In the dining alcove is a built-in corner seat big enough to accommodate four or five at the table, and the dining porch is easily accessible from dining room and kitchen. The latter is large, well lighted and ventilated, and equipped with ample pantry and storage closets, built-in refrigerator and screened entry porch.

The bedrooms, three in number, are located in the attic, but by the use of dormers they are all arranged with full-height ceilings. They are good-sized and have plenty of closet room. The bath and hall linen closet complete the design and form a very compact floor plan.

79

BRICK COTTAGE WITH CONVENIENT BUILT-IN FURNISHINGS

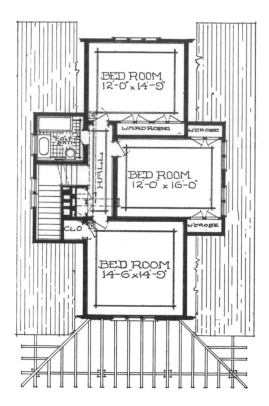

CRAFTSMAN BRICK COTTAGE, NO. 112:
SECOND FLOOR PLAN.

The house may be trimmed throughout the first floor in chestnut, stained a nut brown. The second floor we would trim in gumwood. This wood is beautifully marked with a fine grain, and when stained shows various shades of brown with slight traces of delicate buff and green. Maple floors might be used throughout, finished in a soft shade of gray-brown, a permanent color obtained by the use of vinegar and iron rust, covered with two coats of thin shellac and then waxed.

The view of the interior shown below gives one a good idea of the interesting and somewhat unique arrangement of the living room and dining room. The hospitable charm of the fireside nook with its tiled chimneypiece, built-in bookshelves and seats; the glimpse through the arched alcove of the dining room, with its table and corner seat, and the simple but effective way in which the woodwork, doors and wall spaces are treated,—all these features show what a friendly and homelike atmosphere results from the careful working out of the various structural details. The introduction, too, of Craftsman furnishings and fittings, such as the tables, lamp, hanging and bracket lanterns shown, helps to carry out the effect. Portières which harmonize in color and design with the general decorative scheme of the rooms might be hung across the opening between the living room and entry, to shut off any possible draft from the front door.

LIVING ROOM OF CRAFTSMAN BRICK COTTAGE, NO. 112: GLIMPSE OF FIRESIDE NOOK AND DINING ALCOVE BEYOND.

TWO-STORY HOUSE OF STONE, BRICK AND CEMENT, WITH TYPICAL CRAFTSMAN INTERIOR

Published in The Craftsman, May, 1907.

TWO-STORY CRAFTSMAN HOUSE: NO. 51.

ALTHOUGH the form of this house is straight and square, its rather low, broad proportions and the contrasting materials used in its construction take away all sense of severity. The walls of the lower story and the chimneys are of hard-burned red brick, and the upper walls are of cement plaster with half-timber construction. The foundation steps and porch parapets are of split stone laid up in dark cement, and the roof is tiled. Cement is used for the pillars and also for the floor of the porch.

This is only a suggestion for materials, as the house would be equally well adapted to different forms of construction. The coloring also may be made rich and warm or cool and subdued, as demanded by the surroundings.

One feature that is especially in accordance with Craftsman ideas is the way in which the half-timbers are used. While we do not generally advocate half-timber construction, we believe that when it is used it should be made entirely "probable;" that is, that the timbers should be so placed that they might easily belong to the real construction of the house. Another feature of typical Craftsman construction is illustrated in the windows. It will be noted that they are double-hung in places where they are exposed to the weather, and that casements are used when it is possible to hood them or to place them where they will be sheltered by the roof of the porch.

The arrangement of the interior of this house is very simple, as the living room and dining room, which have merely the suggestion of a dividing partition, occupy the whole of one side. The arrangement of kitchen, hall and staircase on the other side of the house is equally practical, as it utilizes every inch of space and provides many conveniences to lighten the work of the housekeeper.

The entrance door opens into a small vestibule that serves to shut off draughts from the hall, especially as the entrance from the vestibule to the hall is at right angles to the front door instead of being directly opposite, making the danger from drafts so small that this opening might easily be curtained and a second door dispensed with. The broad landing of the staircase is opposite the opening from the vestibule, and in the angle where the stair runs up a large hall seat is built.

DETAIL OF ENTRANCE PORCH: HOUSE NO. 51.

The vestibule jutting into the living room leaves a deep recess at the front, in which is built a long window seat just below the group of casements that appears at the front of the house. The fireplace is in the center of the room just opposite the hall, and another fireplace in the dining room adds to the comfort and cheer.

In a recess in the dining room, somewhat similar to that at the front of the living room, the sideboard is built in so that the front of it is flush with the wall and three casement windows are set just above it. The china cupboards built in on the opposite side are shown in two ways in the plan and illustration. In the former the cupboard is built across the corner, and in the latter it is straight with the wall. Either way would be effective and the choice depends simply upon personal preference and convenience.

CORNER OF LIVING ROOM IN HOUSE NO. 51, AND GLIMPSE OF HALL AND STAIRCASE.

CORNER OF DINING ROOM IN HOUSE NO. 51: THE BUILT-IN FEATURES AND TREATMENT OF WOODWORK MAKE THE INTERIOR OF THIS HOME ESPECIALLY INTERESTING.

TWO-STORY HOUSE WITH TYPICAL CRAFTSMAN INTERIOR

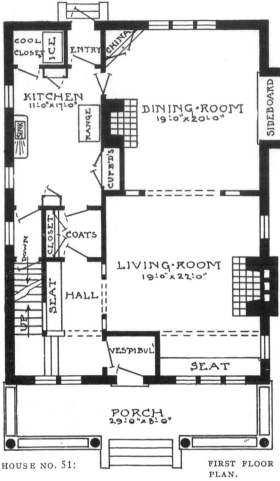

HOUSE NO. 51:   FIRST FLOOR PLAN.

the kitchen. The tiles of the chimneypiece and hearth and the panels of the woodwork seem to carry out still further this unity of effect. In fact, the interior of this house is one which lends itself especially to unusual and interesting treatment of structural features, and a study of the floor plans will reveal many delightful possibilities of furnishing and decoration.

A swinging door leads from the dining room to the kitchen, which is large and provided with ample closet room, including a cool place for the ice-box. A small entry leads to the back door. Between the kitchen and the front hall there is a long closet and plenty of room for coats, umbrellas, etc.

The plan of the second story shows three bedrooms and a bath opening out of the upper hall, which has a small linen closet in one corner. A closet is also provided in each bedroom, and one of the rooms has an open fireplace which utilizes the same chimney that serves for the living room. The two front bedrooms communicate and could be used together if desired, the smaller one serving as dressing room. Or the bedroom with the fireplace could be used as an upstairs sitting room if preferred.

The two views of the living room and dining room shown on page 83 show how effectively the woodwork of the house is used, and how full of friendliness and charm are the various built-in features of the rooms. The paneled wainscot, the simple wall spaces and beams, the post and panel construction between the living room and hall, with the small open space at the top and ledge for plants or pottery, the spindles of the staircase and the small square panes of the casement windows —all harmonize admirably with the Craftsman furniture and fittings shown. The hanging lanterns suspended from the ceiling beam across the recess in the living room are particularly pleasing. In the illustration of the dining room the small panes in the upper portion of the windows are repeated by the doors of the built-in sideboard in the corner, and by the lights in the top of the door leading to

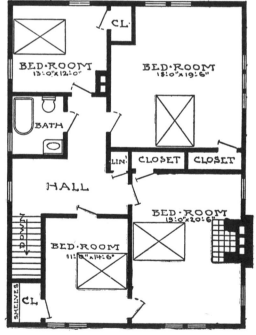

HOUSE NO. 51:   SECOND FLOOR PLAN.

CRAFTSMAN HOUSE OF TAPESTRY BRICK WITH PORCHES, BALCONY AND SPACIOUS INTERIOR

VERY interesting is the use of Tapestry brick in this house. The center of the building, with its balcony of wood, is considerably recessed, leaving the two ends in the form of wings. The floor of this recess may

dining room is filled in the same way with the built-in sideboard and china closets, so that there is hardly a foot of wall space in these rooms that is not treated in a useful and decorative way. At the back of both rooms French

Published in The Craftsman, January, 1911.

TEN-ROOM BRICK HOUSE: NO. 106.

be of dull red cement, and the roof of red slate with tiles at the ridges and angles. At the back of the house are two pergola-covered porches, opening from the living room and the dining room.

The interior view shows an unusually attractive reception hall. Across its entire width runs a huge fireplace nook with a built-in seat at either end. The central fireplace with its copper hood, the tiled walls and floor, the cabinets and recesses above, and the small cupboards with glass doors above the end seats, are all typically Craftsman in effect.

Another fireplace occupies the middle of the outer wall of the living room, and on either side the wall spaces below the casement windows are shelved for books. The end of the

doors open upon the porches, and as windows are placed on either side in the dining room it will be seen that there is ample provision for light and air.

The one-story addition between the two porches at the back of the house gives room for the kitchen, pantry and maid's room, so that the servant's domain is complete in itself and practically cut off from the rest of the house. The service porch is built on the back of the kitchen which is equipped with every convenience for doing housework swiftly and easily.

On the second story the staircase leads into a large central hall lighted from the front by the group of windows which look out upon the balcony and by the glass doors which lead

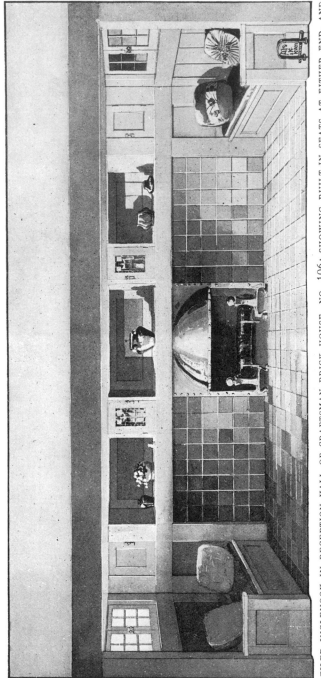

TILED INGLENOOK IN RECEPTION HALL OF CRAFTSMAN BRICK HOUSE, NO. 106: SHOWING BUILT-IN SEATS AT EITHER END, AND DECORATIVE USE OF WALL SPACES FOR CABINETS AND SHELVES.

TEN-ROOM CRAFTSMAN HOUSE OF TAPESTRY BRICK

to it. At the back of this hall is a fireplace nook which, though smaller than the one below, is still large enough to accommodate two comfortable built-in seats. The remainder of the space is occupied by the two bathrooms, one of which serves for the guest chambers at one end of the house, and the other as a private bath for the owner's suite of chamber and dressing room. Such a suite was required in this particular house, but the arrangement might easily be modified to allow two bedrooms instead, as the only al-

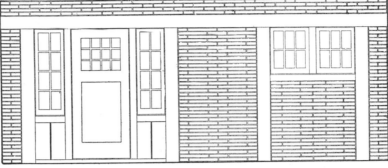

DETAIL ELEVATION OF FRONT WALL AND ENTRANCE DOOR OF BRICK HOUSE, NO. 106.

HOUSE NO. 106.   FIRST FLOOR PLAN.

teration needed would be the omission of the connecting door and the adding of closets between, as in the case of the guest chambers.

An impression of the general effect of the interior of this house can be gained from the illustration on page 86. This shows the tiled inglenook in the reception hall, with its built-in seats and decorative use of wall spaces for cabinets and shelves. Also, a definite idea of the construction of the outer walls of the house and the placing of the doors and window groups, is given by the detail elevation above, which shows the recessed entrance door and the windows on either side. The use of small panes is especially effective, and adds considerably to the interest of the exterior.

A study of the floor plans indicate what a simple task the furnishing of this house would be. The built-in fittings, both upstairs and down, are so numerous that comparatively little movable furniture is required. This not only makes for economy, but simplifies the labor of housekeeping, and adds greatly to the charm of the interior. There is an air of quiet intimacy, of durability and repose about built-in furnishings which brings a restful atmosphere into the home. In this particular case, moreover, the arrangement seems especially typical of the Craftsman ideal. The rooms have a certain spacious hospitality which characterizes most of the Craftsman designs, and at the same time there is plenty of opportunity for privacy when desired. The three large fireplaces, of course, focus much of the interest and increase the comfort of the house, while the porches and balcony permit outdoor life.

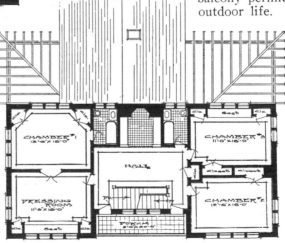

HOUSE NO. 106: SECOND FLOOR PLAN.

BRICK HOUSE WITH MANY HOMELIKE FEATURES

Published in The Craftsman, June, 1909.
REAR VIEW OF BRICK HOUSE WITH SEVEN ROOMS, PERGOLA PORCH AND SLEEPING BALCONIES: NO. 68.

VIEW IN LIVING ROOM OF BRICK HOUSE, NO. 68, SHOWING ARRANGEMENT OF ENTRY AND STAIRCASE.

BRICK HOUSE WITH MANY HOMELIKE FEATURES

THIS house is of brick, with slate roof, exposed rafters and purlins, and pergola-covered porch. The walls of each wing are carried up to form the parapet of a little balcony, fitted with flower-boxes. All the windows in the lower story of the house and those above the roof over the door are casements, opening out.

One enters the house through a vestibule, on one side of which is a toilet, on the other a coat closet, and from the vestibule three steps go up to the living room. The difference in floor levels allows the stairs to the second story to run up over the vestibule, thus economizing space. This arrangement, at once useful and decorative, is clearly shown by the floor plan and the interior view. The latter suggests an interesting use of structural features which, frankly and simply treated, have a distinct decorative value, and become an important factor in the general effectiveness of the rooms. The plain lines of

the woodwork, the unpretentious charm of the entrance door, with the small windows on either side, the bench beside the staircase, the lamp of the newel post,—all these features convey an idea of the general treatment of the rest of the interior.

The living room is large and is lighted by groups of windows and a glass door which gives access to the long porch at the rear of the house. Beyond the living room, in the wing, is the den, which is provided, like the living room, with an open fireplace. A long seat is built in beside the hearth and below the rear windows, as the floor plan shows.

On the opposite side of the living room is the dining room with its open fireplace and built-in group of sideboard and china closets. Swing doors lead through the pantry to the kitchen, which is compact and convenient in arrangement.

There are three bedrooms on the second floor, two of them having open fireplaces, and one, built-in seats.

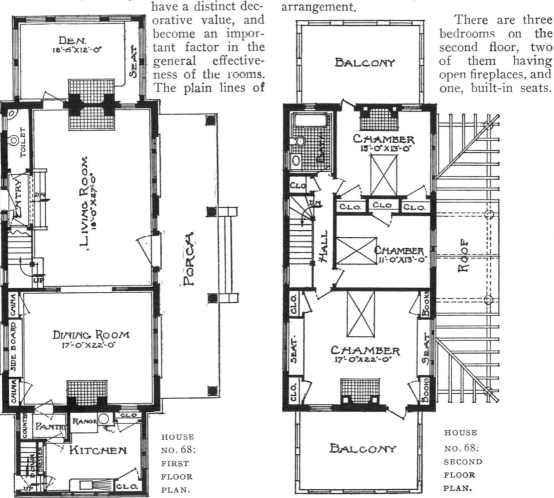

HOUSE NO. 68: FIRST FLOOR PLAN.

HOUSE NO. 68: SECOND FLOOR PLAN.

CITY HOUSE WITH INTERESTING FAÇADE AND SLEEPING BALCONY, AND HOMELIKE INTERIOR

WE are showing here a house of Craftsman construction with open, simple interior and yet adapted to a restricted space and suited to life in the city. The house is planned to be built on a long, narrow lot, 25 feet wide. As the floor plans show, the building is semi-detached, having on one side a party wall, while on the other the windows are arranged to overlook a side court or alley. The arrangement of the rooms, therefore, is considerably modified by the limited space allowed and the necessarily long, narrow shape of the building, and the exterior is modified to an even greater degree, because, as the house is not intended to be built on a corner lot, the façade is all that can be seen from the street.

As it was manifestly impossible to introduce any of the features that make up the beauty and comfort of a country house, we have sought a new expression of our basic architectural principles.

Richly-colored, rough-surfaced Tapestry bricks are used, laid in darkened mortar with wide joints. The main roof, the dormer roof, the hood over the entrance door and the upper part of the pilasters are all dull green matt-glazed tile. The porch is screened by flower-boxes.

Published in The Craftsman, October, 1910.

THREE-STORY CRAFTSMAN HOUSE FOR THE CITY, WITH SLEEPING BAL-CONY AND HOMELIKE INTERIOR: NO. 99.

THREE-STORY CRAFTSMAN HOUSE FOR THE CITY

ONE END OF A BEDROOM IN HOUSE NO. 99, SHOWING TREATMENT OF WOODWORK, DOORS AND WINDOWS.

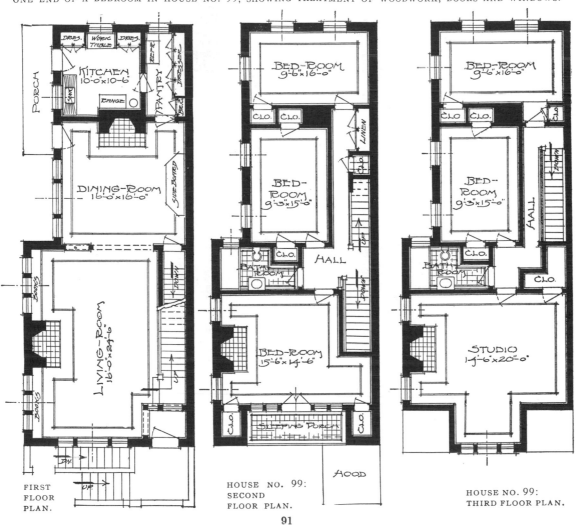

FIRST
FLOOR
PLAN.

HOUSE NO. 99:
SECOND
FLOOR PLAN.

HOUSE NO. 99:
THIRD FLOOR PLAN.

CRAFTSMAN CITY HOUSE WITH SECOND-STORY PORCH AND THIRD-STORY SLEEPING BALCONY

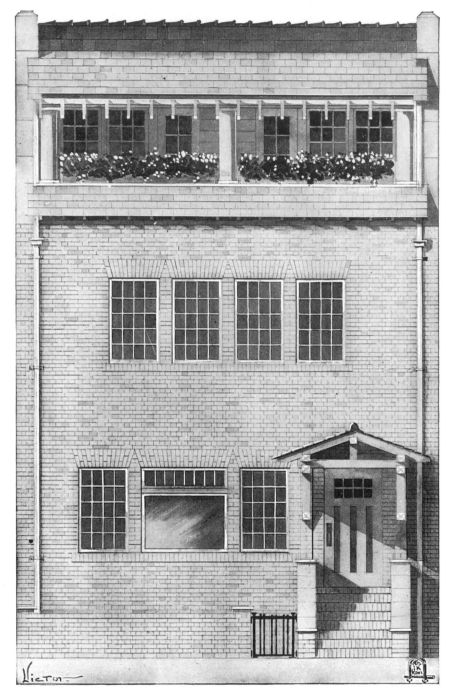

Published in The Craftsman, October, 1910.

CRAFTSMAN BRICK HOUSE FOR THE CITY, WITH ELEVEN ROOMS AND TWO SLEEPING PORCHES: NO. 100.

ELEVEN-ROOM CITY HOUSE, WITH TWO SLEEPING PORCHES

LIKE the house shown on pages 91 and 92, this building is also planned for a 25-foot city lot. But the restrictions in this case are even greater, for instead of facing an alley on one side the central portion of this house obtains light and ventilation from an interior court or air-shaft on which the windows of library, dining room, bathroom and several bedrooms open. Notwithstanding this fact, the careful planning of the interior insures light and air for all the rooms.

Plain red hard-burned brick is used for the façade, the uniform dark red being varied by the darker purplish tones of the arch brick which are introduced wherever they will be effective. The roof and the hood over the entrance door are of dull red tile.

The object being to get a good design and construction as inexpensively as possible, the sleeping porch is placed on the third story just under the tiled roof. The rafters of the roof are emphasized, projecting sufficiently to give a suggestion of a pergola and affording a support for vines that might be grown in the flower-boxes.

The half-tone illustration of the staircase in the living room shows the way in which the stairs are screened by a high-backed seat and an arrangement of slats above. The fireplace in the large back bedroom is also shown, with

TWO VIEWS OF INTERIOR OF CITY HOUSE, NO. 100. THE FIRST SHOWS STAIRWAY GOING UP FROM LIVING ROOM, WITH BUILT-IN SEAT AND SPINDLES ABOVE; THE SECOND SHOWS FIREPLACE END OF ONE OF THE BEDROOMS, WITH GLASS DOORS ON EACH SIDE LEADING TO SLEEPING PORCH.

ELEVEN-ROOM CITY HOUSE, WITH TWO SLEEPING PORCHES

the glass doors on either side opening upon the rear porch.

The floor plans show the front entrance door opening directly into the living room, which has a large open fireplace on one side. By placing corner seats or long settles beside the hearth a very comfortable inglenook could be formed. Beyond this room is the library, with a window group in one wall overlooking the interior court, and on the opposite side are built-in bookshelves with windows set high in the wall above. Beyond the library is the dining room with its open fireplace, on the right

of which is a swing door leading to the conveniently arranged kitchen in the rear.

The second floor contains three bedrooms and bath, with ample closet room. On each side of the fireplace in the back bedroom are doors leading to the porch. On the third floor are four bedrooms and a bath. Here also there are plenty of closets. The two front rooms open upon the recessed sleeping porch, with its pleasant screen of flower-boxes. This porch has a partition across the center as shown, and is so sheltered from the weather that it could be used practically all the year round.

While city restrictions have not permitted a typical Craftsman dwelling, still the house reveals many possibilities for the making of a comfortable and homelike interior.

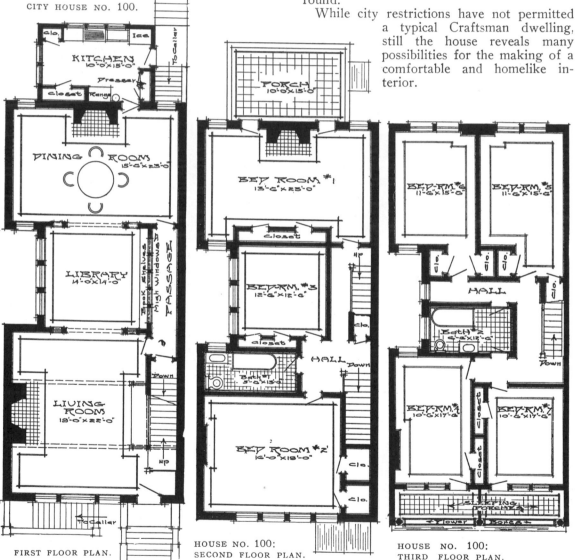

CITY HOUSE NO. 100.

FIRST FLOOR PLAN.

HOUSE NO. 100: SECOND FLOOR PLAN.

HOUSE NO. 100: THIRD FLOOR PLAN.

INEXPENSIVE COTTAGE FOR A SMALL FAMILY

Published in The Craftsman, December, 1910.   COTTAGE OF BRICK, CLAPBOARD AND SHINGLE: NO. 103.

WHILE the cost has been carefully kept down to the minimum for a properly built Craftsman house, this little dwelling is solidly made as well as comfortable and attractive. It is planned for a family of not more than two or three people. It would be entirely suitable for the first home of a newly married couple just starting in life, or for a man and wife whose children are all married and gone and who wish to pass the remainder of their lives in a snug little home that gives the least possible trouble to the housekeeper. Or, it would be convenient for two self-supporting women who might revolt at the ordinary flat or boarding-house existence and pool their resources to build a home of their own.

The walls of this house are built of brick according to a method of construction which is both economical and practically fireproof. The gables are sheathed with wide cypress boards, V-jointed and darkened so that they show the natural reddish brown color and strong markings of the wood. The square pillars of the front porch are made of brick like the wall, and the main roof is shingled and

stained to a warm brown tone that harmonizes with the brick and with the boarding of the gables. The roof of the dormer, being neces-

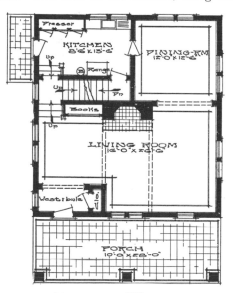

COTTAGE NO. 103: FIRST FLOOR PLAN.

sarily much flatter than the main roof in order to allow head room in the chambers on the

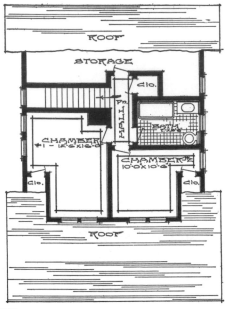

upper floor, is not sufficiently steep in pitch to be shingled; therefore, it is covered with Ruberoid, the upper edge of which runs to the ridge-pole beneath the top courses of shingles which extend the entire length of the roof, forming a finish at the top for the dormer roof. This Ruberoid is painted the same color as the roof shingles, and may be battened or not according to taste. The rafters supporting it are left exposed.

The front door opens into a small vestibule which is little more than a recess in the living room. The end of this vestibule serves to hold a coat closet and the partition wall gives to the living room a "jog" that breaks up what would be otherwise a plain square in shape. The fireplace is directly in the center and the dining room is as much a part of the main room as is usual in a Craftsman house.

The kitchen, though very small, is equipped with conveniences which should make the housework easy to handle. Upstairs there are two bedrooms, a bathroom and a large storage room under the slope of the roof at the back of the house.

CORNER OF DINING ROOM IN CRAFTSMAN BRICK COTTAGE, NO. 103.

MODERATE-SIZED BRICK HOUSE, WITH RECESSED PORCH AND PLEASANT, HOMELIKE ROOMS

Published in The Craftsman, December, 1910.

SEVEN-ROOM BRICK HOUSE: NO. 104.

THE walls of this house are of brick, constructed in such a manner that they are both economical and practically fireproof. The gables show a sheathing of V-jointed boards. The round pillars of the porch are painted white, serving with the window sash to relieve the subdued color scheme of the house.

One interesting structural feature is seen in the posts which frame the entrance door and form the corners of the small vestibule. These are solid square timbers and the bricks between are laid up just as they are in the walls, giving a construction that is really what it appears to be instead of the ordinary half-timber construction which shows merely strips of wood nailed on the outside. The roof is of rough-finished slate, preferably dark red in color, and the ridge-pole is of tile. The porch, which extends down one side, is floored with cement.

The whole end of the living room is occupied by the big fireplace nook shown in the illustration. This forms the chief structural

feature of the house and also gives the keynote of color. The hearth, which extends over the entire nook, is paved with red tiles, and built-in

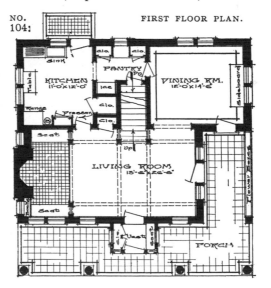

97

COMPACT SEVEN-ROOM HOUSE, WITH RECESSED PORCH

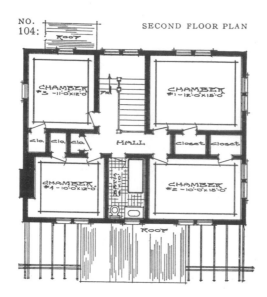

NO. 104: SECOND FLOOR PLAN

hard-burned red brick with cement above, finished in a tone that harmonizes with both the brick and the walls. The walls in this room are wainscoted up to the ceiling with chestnut boards, and the ceiling is crossed by massive beams.

The stairs lead up from the living room, with closet and kitchen door on one side, and on the other a wide opening into the dining room. The latter is lighted by two double casement windows and a glass door leading onto the sheltered porch. A similar door, with windows on either side, leads from the porch into the living room. This recessed corner of the porch, which is further screened by a side parapet and flower-boxes, would make a delightful outdoor dining room.

Both kitchen and pantry are compactly arranged, with ample closet room, and the kitchen range uses the same chimney as the living-room fireplace.

The upper floor affords space for four chambers, with plenty of closet room and a bath. These rooms are of moderate size and very simple in shape, being arranged to afford the greatest amount of space possible in a house of these dimensions.

seats on either side offer a delightful suggestion of home comfort, particularly as the wall spaces flanking the chimneypiece are shelved for books, and the whole nook is lighted by small casement windows set high in the wall. The chimneypiece up to the mantelshelf is

VIEW OF RECESSED INGLENOOK IN HOUSE NO. 104, WITH BRICK AND CEMENT CHIMNEYPIECE, TILED HEARTH. BUILT-IN BOOKSHELVES AND SEATS AND CASEMENT WINDOWS.

RURAL ONE-STORY BUNGALOW OF FIELD STONE

Published in The Craftsman, November, 1908.

ONE-STORY CRAFTSMAN BUNGALOW: NO. 55.

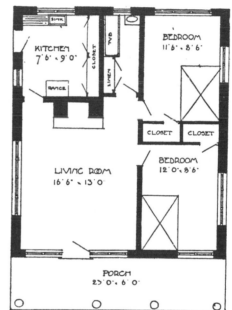

FLOOR PLAN OF STONE BUNGALOW, NO. 55.

THIS little cottage is planned and constructed on simple and practical lines. The walls and chimney are built of field stone. There is a regular bungalow roof, low-pitched, square in line and widely overhanging. This extends in front of the house without a break over the porch and is supported by the log pillars that belong so definitely to this type of building.

The entrance door leads directly from the porch into the living room, which is a comfortable size and is provided with an open fireplace so placed that it serves to warm the adjacent rooms. There are windows on each side of the entrance door as well as along the other outer wall of the living room, and the two bedrooms and kitchen are also well lighted and ventilated. Each of these latter rooms is provided with a closet, and a linen closet is also included in the bathroom. As in the other bungalows, the arrangement here is as simple as it is convenient.

The detail view given here of the entrance to the bungalow shows what effective charm lies in this simple construction. The stone walls, the plain wood door, with its long iron hinges, the small-paned casement windows on either hand, the square-tiled floor of the porch and the flower-boxes at the side, all seem perfectly in keeping with the character and purpose of this little rural home.

The cost of construction would be comparatively low.

DETAIL OF ENTRANCE TO BUNGALOW, NO. 55.

ONE-STORY CRAFTSMAN BUNGALOW PLANNED ON SIMPLE AND ECONOMIC LINES

Published in The Craftsman, September, 1909.   FIVE-ROOM BUNGALOW: NO. 75.

THE bungalow shown here seems particularly suitable for a rural site. Split field stone is used for the foundation and for the walls of the porch. The sides of the building above this are shingled, and the gables are covered with V-jointed boards. The round pillars supporting the porch are shown of cement, but posts of hewn wood might be used instead. The harmonious variety of these materials, the ample porch, the interesting windows and broad slope of the roof give the exterior an air of hospitality and repose that is very homelike.

The plans show the rooms to be conveniently arranged so that, although on the same floor, the bedrooms are completely separated from the kitchen and living room. The latter serves also as the dining room and is a large apartment occupying almost one-third of the whole bungalow. It opens upon the porch by a glass door, on either side of which is a window group consisting of two single casements with a stationary glass panel between. Above these windows are transoms set with small panes— a very attractive arrangement and an additional method of ventilation. A large portion of the end wall is devoted to windows, and indeed so much light and sunshine come to the room that it is almost a sun parlor.

The interior of this bungalow, which was

built in nineteen hundred and nine, was decorated in Craftsman style. The tones in hammered copper seemed best to sum up the light and shade that were needed in the rooms, and our color scheme accordingly resolved itself into an analysis of these hues.

The walls were left in brown plaster with no finishing surface applied. Against this tone were the girders, the built-in sideboard and all the stationary woodwork of chestnut, the sunny, variegated browns of which furnished a transition from the light tone of the walls to the deep red-brown of the fumed oak furniture, upholstered in leather of the same shade. The wood furniture was varied by occasional pieces of brownish green willow which blended the brown of the furniture and walls with the green rug on the floor. The design in the rug was worked out in dull amber and red-brown, and these shades were repeated in the lanterns of hammered copper set with amber glass and suspended by chains from the girders. The china-closet doors had panes of this same glass, and, like the sideboard, the trim was of hammered copper. The chimneypiece was of split field stone, with a thick board shelf, and the hearth was set with square, rough-textured tiles blending with the color of the rug and of the stone.

The large bedroom in the front of the bun-

100

LIVING ROOM IN BUNGALOW NO. 75: A HOMELIKE CRAFTSMAN INTERIOR.

galow has two corner closets with a seat built into the recess formed between them. Over the seat is a group of windows which overlook the porch,—a stationary panel in the center and an outward opening casement on each side. The other two bedrooms are each provided with a closet, and there is also one in the small hall beside the bathroom. The kitchen is compactly planned, with range and dresser on one side and tubs, sink and drainboard on the other. On one side of the rear entry is the ice-box, and on the other the door to the cellar stairs.

The view of the interior will serve to give some impression of the homelike and artistic quality of the rooms of this little bungalow.

CRAFTS-MAN CANDLE-STICK SHOWN IN INTERIOR OF BUNGALOW NO. 75.

BUNGALOW FLOOR PLAN: NO. 75.

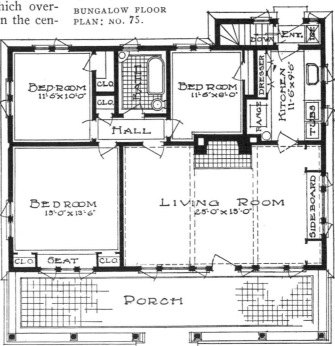

TWO-STORY COUNTRY BUNGALOW MADE COMFORTABLE WITH MUCH BUILT-IN FURNITURE

Published in The Craftsman, October, 1909.

SEVEN-ROOM BUNGALOW: NO. 76.

IN planning this two-story bungalow a variation of ten feet was found in the elevation of the site, and this has been met by a series of rough terraces in keeping with the rugged character of the vicinity. Although designed for a hillside situation, the broad low lines of the structure adapt it equally well to a level suburban site. The foundation is of stone, the siding is of rived shingles left to weather, and the roof of rough slate with a tile ridge.

As the object has been to bring as much outdoor feeling as possible into the house, especial attention has been given to the windows, of which there are a great many.

The living room occupies the center of the house. The rear end is used as the dining room, with double French doors leading out under a pergola. On either side are casement windows, so that the end of the room is largely glass. Beneath the casements two useful pieces of furniture are constructed: combination sideboards and china closets. The front wall of the room is also chiefly windows, and the proportions of the big stationary panel with its ventilating transom of small panes

contrast pleasantly with the sizes of the casements. This end of the room projects between twin porches and is connected with them by French doors.

The chimneypiece in this room is one of its chief beauties. It is of split field stone with a rough tiled hearth and board shelf. The opening for the fire is five feet high, so that the logs may be stood upon end, and the effect of

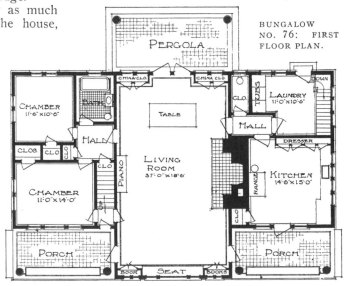

BUNGALOW NO. 76: FIRST FLOOR PLAN.

ONE END OF LIVING ROOM IN BUNGALOW NO. 76. ON EACH SIDE OF THE GLASS DOORS THAT LEAD OUT ONTO THE PERGOLA ARE BUILT-IN CHINA CLOSETS AND DRAWERS, WITH CASEMENT WINDOWS ABOVE.

the firelight upon the depth of the chimney-piece is very beautiful and unusual. We have rarely designed a room that could be so effectively furnished with so little trouble.

On one side of the fireplace is a door leading to a small hallway which communicates with closet, laundry and kitchen. The latter opens onto the corner porch. On the other side of the living room is a second hall, communicating with two bedrooms and the bathroom. Each bedroom has a closet and there are also two in the hall.

As the floor plans show, this arrangement of the rooms is very practical, the service portion of the house being grouped on one side of the central living room, quite apart from the rest, and the sleeping apartments being equally separate on the opposite side of the bungalow. Thus there is the greatest possible convenience and privacy, and at the same time the large middle room furnishes a hospitable gathering place for family and guests. So far as this room is concerned, the built-in fittings will help to minimize both the cost of furnishing and the amount of housework need to keep it in order,

besides adding to the general comfort of the interior by its air of permanence and repose.

The view of the living room gives a general idea of the interior, and it will be noticed that the use of small panes in the long glass doors, casement windows and cabinet doors gives a pleasant effect of trelliswork in the room.

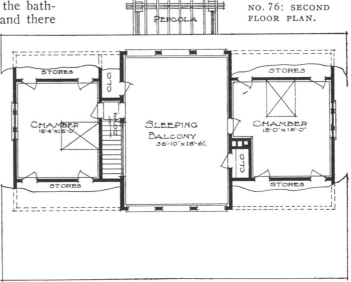

BUNGALOW NO. 76: SECOND FLOOR PLAN.

THIS SKETCH SHOWS ARRANGEMENT OF FRONT WALL OF LIVING ROOM IN BUNGALOW NO. 76, WITH LONG BUILT-IN WINDOW SEAT BETWEEN THE BOOKCASES, AND GLASS DOOR AT THE LEFT OPENING ONTO ONE OF THE FRONT PORCHES.

The sleeping balcony is intended to be used in all sorts of weather, and a flight of stairs connects it directly with the chamber on the first floor and with the living room. On either side of the sleeping balcony, which is protected by dormer roofs, are two large rooms which may be fitted with hammocks and bunks or finished into the more usual style of sleeping room. There is ample closet room beneath the slope of the roof, both in front and rear.

CHIMNEYPIECE OF SPLIT FIELD STONE AND ROUGH TILED HEARTH IN LIVING ROOM OF BUNGALOW NO. 76.

SHINGLED HOUSE WITH SPACIOUS LIVING ROOM AND SHELTERED PORCHES

THIS house is of shingle construction and the whole of one end is taken up with the recessed porch and sleeping balcony above. The small entrance porch is sheltered by a shingled hood supported on brackets, and small across the wide opening of the living room, and the posts that define the opening into the dining room. The walls in both rooms are wainscoted to the height of the frieze with V-jointed boards, and the frames of doors

Published in The Craftsman, June, 1910　　　　　SEVEN-ROOM SHINGLED HOUSE: NO. 92.

hoods appear over each of the windows that are exposed to the weather, and also over the openings at the ends of the upper and lower porches.

This building is simple in form and the arrangement of the lower story is very open, giving the effect of more space than would seem possible, considering the size of the house. The living room occupies the whole depth of the building. A big chimneypiece is built in the middle of the outside wall, the chimney projecting on both porch and balcony. On either side of this chimneypiece is a glass door leading to the porch, with windows on each side. Grouped windows also appear at either end of the room, so that it is well lighted and cheerful. The entrance door opens into a small vestibule, which leads in turn into a hallway connecting the dining room and living room. The position of this hallway is hardly more than indicated by the staircase, the ceiling beam

and windows are so planned that they appear merely to emphasize the construction of the wainscot. The living

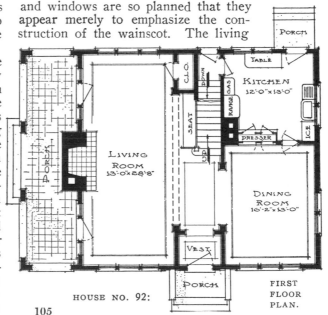

HOUSE NO. 92:　　　FIRST FLOOR PLAN.

SEVEN-ROOM SHINGLED HOUSE WITH SHELTERED PORCHES

room is also fitted with a closet and a long built-in seat beside the staircase.

The interior view below gives some impression of the generous dimensions of this room, and the sense of light and airiness that results from the numerous and pleasantly grouped windows. The stone fireplace in the center of the long wall adds a homelike and hospitable note.

From the dining room a swing door leads into the kitchen, which includes among its furnishings a dresser to which access may be had from both these rooms.

The second floor is divided into four bedrooms, bathroom and hall, each room, as well as the hall, being provided with a closet. The hall and stairs are lighted by a window in the rear wall of the house just above the landing.

The two bedrooms at the right have double windows in both outer walls, and the two rooms on the opposite side of the house, in addition to the windows in front and rear, have glass doors opening onto the long sleeping balcony which extends across the side of the house above the lower porch. This balcony is well sheltered from the weather, and if further protected with awnings could be used practically all the year. If desired, of course, a parti-

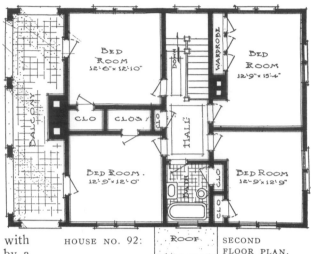

HOUSE NO. 92: SECOND FLOOR PLAN.

tion could be placed across the center to divide it into two private outdoor sleeping apartments.

This house, unlike most of the Craftsman designs, shows very few built-in fittings, the furnishing being left to the taste of the owner. The lower floor plan, however, could be very comfortably arranged, with fireside seats either in front of the hearth or on either side of it, and bookcases in the corners of the room. In the dining room there is plenty of space left for sideboard and china closets, and a window seat could also be included.

INTERESTING EXAMPLE OF DOOR AND WINDOW GROUPING IN LIVING ROOM OF HOUSE NO. 92.

COMFORTABLE SHINGLED HOUSE WITH BUILT-IN FITTINGS AND SLEEPING PORCHES

Published in The Craftsman, November, 1910.

CRAFTSMAN SHINGLED HOUSE: NO. 101.

A SHINGLED house with Ruberoid roof is shown here—simple in design, compact in arrangement, and comparatively inexpensive as regards the cost of construction. The interior is economical to a degree, the floor space being utilized to the best advantage and the plumbing and heating facilities planned to cost as little as possible. One large central chimney serves for the whole house.

The wide porch, floored with cement, extends across the front of the building. The living room also extends the whole width of the house, and is entered by two glass doors. The wall space between these doors is occu-

BUILT-IN TABLE IN LIVING ROOM: HOUSE NO. 101.

LIVING-ROOM FIREPLACE IN HOUSE NO. 101.

pied by two small coat closets which project into the room, and in the recess between these closets a table is built, with a shelf below and windows in the wall above. Directly opposite is the big recessed fireplace of split stone.

Illustrations are given on page 107 of both the built-in table and the fireplace. The view of the former shows the compactness of arrangement, the effective treatment of wainscot and paneled doors, and the use of small square panes in the upper portion of the latter, repeating the larger panes of the windows. The view of the fireplace shows how much is added to the charm of the stonework by the arched recess with its long shelf. A comfortable seat could be placed directly opposite the fireplace, or if preferred, settles might be used on either side of the hearth, thus forming a sort of inglenook.

Turning again to the floor plans, at the left of the living room we find the entire wall filled by a wide couch beneath the windows and built-in bookcases on either side. Besides being a very comfortable and convenient arrangement, this adds much to the structural interest of the interior. The wainscot is of V-jointed boards to the height of the frieze, and the ceiling beams extending across the room from the fireplace to the closets in the opposite wall emphasize the frankness and simplicity of the construction, and at the same time give one a slight sense of separation be-

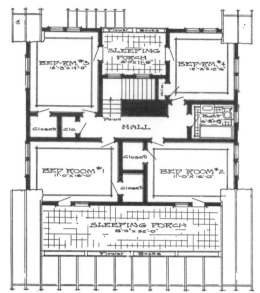

HOUSE NO. 101: SECOND FLOOR PLAN.

tween the fireplace portion and the ends of the room. Each end of the living room is lighted with a group of windows, and at the right of the fireplace the opening into the dining room is so wide that it allows only the post and panel construction on either side.

Almost the entire side of the dining room is occupied by a group of windows like that in the living room, and the whole end is filled with built-in china closets and sideboard. The staircase goes up from the dining room just back of the fireplace, a rather unusual arrangement made necessary by the plan of the house. A large pantry, well equipped, is placed between the dining room and kitchen, and the latter, though rather small, affords all facilities for housework.

Each one of the four bedrooms communicates with a sleeping porch. The front porch is open to the sky except for the slight shelter afforded by the eaves of the dormer. Yet it is so shielded by being sunk, as it were, in the main roof, that it is wholly sheltered from observation below. Flower-boxes along the front add to this sense of privacy, and the rise of the roof serves all the purposes of a wall at either end. The recessed and sheltered porch at the back could be easily glassed in for a sun room during winter, and if properly heated such a room would make a delightful sewing room or upstairs sitting room—almost a necessity in a house like this, where the lower story is so open.

HOUSE NO. 101:   FIRST FLOOR PLAN.

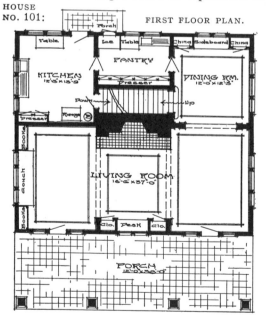

SHINGLED HOUSE WITH AMPLE PROVISION FOR OUTDOOR LIVING

Published in The Craftsman, November, 1910.

NINE-ROOM SHINGLED HOUSE: NO. 102

IN this house shingles are used for the walls and Ruberoid for the roof. There is a comparatively small porch covered by a pergola in front of the house, but at the back there is plenty of room for outdoor life. The porch opening from the living room is as large as the room itself, and is intended to be used as an outdoor living room in summer and as a sun room in winter. The other porch might be used as an outdoor dining room or given over to the maid, whose room looks out upon it. The maid's room in this house is placed next to the kitchen, because we have had so many requests from housekeepers for such an arrangement. The room connects with both the kitchen and the pantry, and through the pantry with the porch.

The front door opens directly into the large central hall, but is screened by the arrangement shown in the elevation. On the floor plan this is called an entry, but all that separates it from the living room is a high-backed seat with a screen of spindles above extending to the ceiling. This gives the same effect as a sofa or settle set out into the room, and yet shuts off the front door as much as is necessary. This seat faces the fireplace, and heavy beams running across the ceiling bind

WAINSCOTED AND SPINDLED SEAT FACING HALL FIREPLACE IN HOUSE NO. 102.

FIREPLACE AND GLIMPSE OF STAIRWAY BEHIND, IN HALL OF HOUSE NO. 102.

with a row of windows set high, and bookshelves are built below. At the opposite end of the vista appear the sideboard and c h i n a closets, which occupy the whole end of the dining room. Wide groups of windows light both rooms from the front, and both open with glass doors to the porches in the rear.

There are four bedrooms on the second floor and two sleeping porches which may be used for outdoor bedrooms in mild weather and glassed in during the winter. These porches are open only at one end.

In the two front bedrooms there is an especially convenient arrangement of closets and window seat, the closets occupying the corners and the seat being built in the recess formed between them. One of these rooms has a private bath, the other bathroom opening out of the hall. In this hall two linen closets are provided.

This floor plan, of course, could be modified to suit various requirements. For instance, if a second bath were not needed, the space could be used for a small dressing room in connection with the corner bedroom. Or it could be included in the middle room.

the two together and define the intention of the arrangement. Two other beams serve to mark the division from the living room on one side and from the dining room on the other, but the openings into both these rooms are so wide that the effect is that of one long room. At one side of the fireplace is a coat closet, with the door concealed in the wainscot, and on the other side is the stair landing. The staircase itself runs up back of the fireplace. An arrangement that is especially convenient is the carrying of the smoke-pipe from the kitchen range underneath this staircase in a terra cotta flue. This prevents any possibility of danger, utilizes the central chimney for the range as well as the fireplace, and does away with any disfigurement.

The entire end of the living room is lighted

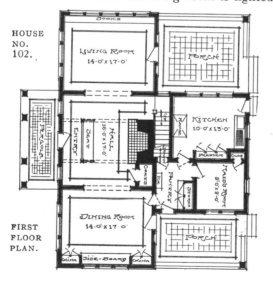

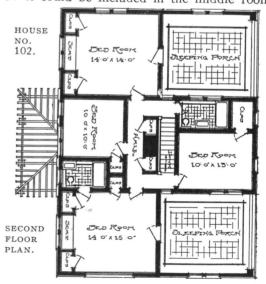

SHINGLED COTTAGE SUITABLE FOR COUNTRY, SEASIDE OR SUBURBAN LIFE

Published in The Craftsman, November, 1909.

SEVEN-ROOM SHINGLED COTTAGE: NO. 78.

THIS little cottage, ideal for the seaside but adapted also to suburban or country building, is covered with rived shingles. Where the windows are not sheltered by the overhanging roof they are protected by springing the shingles out over the head of the windows into the form of a hood which acts as a watershed and prevents the rain and moisture from lodging about the casings.

The shingles, if of split cypress, may be left to weather to the silvery gray color of driftwood, or given a wash of diluted sulphuric acid which will slightly burn the surface to a dull brown. In the chimney the varying tones of the field stone and the red of the brick will add color and interest to the exterior, and the roof may be stained a dull green or red, giving a touch of brightness to the landscape.

The interior is very compactly planned. The living room with its big stone fireplace occupies one whole side of the house. The ceiling shows two of the heavy structural beams. At the rear end of the room is a

low bookcase and at the opposite end a long, deep seat is built in beneath the windows. The dining room, as shown in the

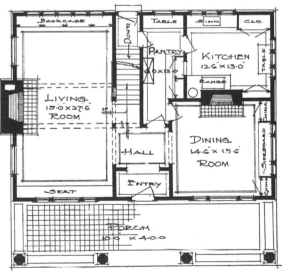

COTTAGE NO. 78: FIRST FLOOR PLAN.

111

COTTAGE FOR COUNTRY, SEASIDE OR SUBURBS

drawing of the interior, contains a built-in sideboard with a cupboard, and a china closet on either side. The stairs lead up from the rear of the hall, which is practically a part of the living room. Note the opening with a lattice frame which makes an attractive setting for a pot of flowers. At the foot of the stairs a door is seen which opens into a rear hall, connecting with a large and convenient pantry. The kitchen is well fitted with closets and a big dresser. The second floor is divided into four airy bedrooms with a bath at the end of the hall. One of these bedrooms has an open fireplace with a closet on one side, and in the recess formed by the front dormer there is a long seat built in beneath the window group. A similar seat is provided in the dormer nook in the other front bedroom, and also in one of the rooms at the rear. The front bedroom on the left has ample closet room beneath the slope of the roof, and the other rooms have closets against the interior walls. There is also a linen closet in the hall.

The somewhat irregular shape of the bedrooms will add to the interest of their furnishing.

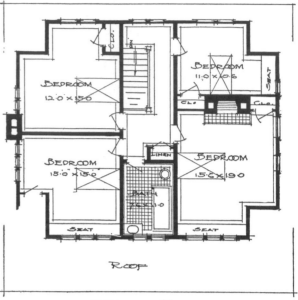

COTTAGE NO. 78: SECOND FLOOR PLAN.

VIEW FROM LIVING ROOM OF COTTAGE NO. 78, WITH GLIMPSE OF STAIRCASE, HALL AND DINING ROOM BEYOND.

112

PRACTICAL SIX-ROOM SHINGLED COTTAGE

Published in The Craftsman, March, 1910.

SIX-ROOM SHINGLED COTTAGE: NO. 86.

THE walls and roof of this cottage are shingled, the porch pillars are peeled and hewn logs, and the porch floor is cement.

The open hearth and fireside seat, the built-in sideboard in the dining room and the bookcases between the rooms are pleasant features of the interior.

Upstairs the dormer nook in each front bedroom is so deep that it might even serve as a small extra room, for the couch built in below the window is meant to serve as a bed if needed. Or the bedroom proper might be arranged as a sitting room, and the couch in the nook used regularly as a bed.

FIRST FLOOR PLAN: NO. 86.

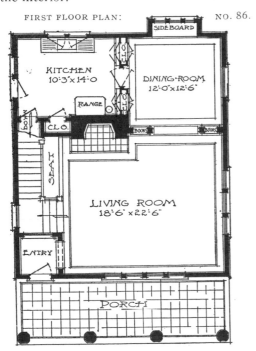

SECOND FLOOR PLAN: NO. 86.

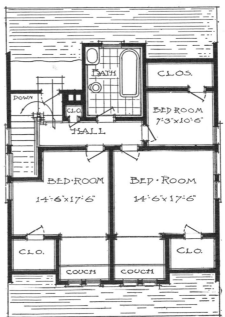

SMALL CRAFTSMAN FARMHOUSE OF STONE AND SHINGLES, SIMPLE AND HOMELIKE IN DESIGN

Published in The Craftsman, February, 1909.

SIX-ROOM FARMHOUSE: NO. 61

VILLAGE or open country would be the environment most suitable for this little house. The walls are shingled and the low foundation is of field stone, sunk into a site that has not been too carefully leveled off. This irregularity of the ground is utilized in a practical way, the slope at the back being sufficient to allow space for the cellar windows, while at the front it is high enough to bring the cement floor of the porch almost upon a level with the lawn. Instead of parapets, the spaces between the pillars of the porch are filled with long flower-boxes which serve as a slight screen and add a note of color to the house. The roof extends over the porch and the sweep of it is broken by the dormer with its group of casements which give light to both bedrooms and the sewing room.

The entrance door at the corner of the porch opens directly into a little nook in the living room. Directly opposite the door is the stairway which runs up three steps to a square landing and then turns and goes up behind the wainscoted wall of the room. The whole wall on this side is taken up by the long fireside seat. The chimneypiece of split field stone occupies the space between the wall and the opening into the dining room. This little ingle-

nook is shown in the illustration which gives some idea of the treatment of the wainscot, posts and beams. A decorative note is added by the Craftsman hanging lanterns above. Behind the dining room is a small, conveniently arranged kitchen.

Upstairs there are two bedrooms, a tiny sewing room, bathroom and hall. Both bedrooms communicate with the sewing room which is placed between them and is provided with a wardrobe. There is ample closet room at each corner beneath the slope of the roof, and one of the bedrooms also has a closet with shelves against the inner wall beside the central chimney. Seats are built into the front recesses beneath the windows.

The house is a small one, having only five rooms and bath, but the compactness of its arrangement and the sense of space given by the openness of the lower floor plan result in a very homelike interior.

For the farmer who is planning to build a home of his own, the farmhouse shown here, as well as those on other pages of the book, should prove full of practical and helpful suggestions in arrangement and design. We have endeavored to keep the plans as simple and inexpensive as possible, and at the same

114

SMALL CRAFTSMAN FARMHOUSE OF STONE AND SHINGLES

STONE FIREPLACE IN CORNER OF LIVING ROOM OF FARMHOUSE NO. 61, WITH FIRESIDE SEAT AND GLIMPSE OF STAIRCASE.

time to secure the greatest possible comfort and beauty, both in the exterior of the building and the rooms within. For the farmer has tolerated too long the discomfort and bareness of the average farmhouse. He needs a home for himself and his family which is both comfortable and cheerful, a place where he may find rest and recreation after the day's work, and in which the necessary labor of the household may be done under conditions which make it as light as possible.

When our farmhouses are designed from this standpoint of utility and beauty, we shall no longer regard the work within their walls as a round of drudgery, a necessary evil. Instead, the so-called "menial" tasks of cooking, sweeping, sewing, will be a source of pleasure and pride, and in place of the old weary attitude toward work we shall find ourselves laboring with interest, with enthusiasm,—qualities which are inevitable in the building up of the ideal home.

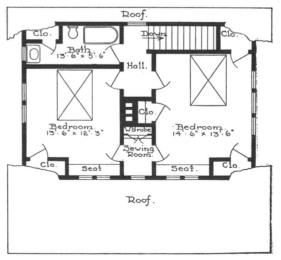

FARMHOUSE NO. 61: FIRST FLOOR PLAN.

FARMHOUSE NO. 61: SECOND FLOOR PLAN.

CRAFTSMAN RURAL DWELLING COMBINING BEAUTY, COMFORT AND CONVENIENCE

Published in The Craftsman, March, 1909.

THIS farmhouse is designed with simple lines, clapboarded or shingled walls and a broad sheltering roof, the straight sweep of which is broken by a large dormer on either side. The interior arrangement is very simple, as there is hardly anything to mark a division between the reception hall, the long living room with its fireplace nook, and the dining room. The arrangement of space avoids all sense of bareness, and if wood in the form of beams and wainscots is liberally used the effect will be friendly and homelike. The kind of wood selected would naturally depend upon the locality, and a safe rule to follow in nearly every case is the use of local materials so far as practicable. The color scheme, of course, would be based upon the tone of the wood.

The front door, which is extremely simple in design, opens from the porch into a small entry which in turn opens into the wide reception hall. The center of interest of the room is, of course the wide inglenook with its stone chimneypiece and fireside seat.

The interior view shows the arrangement of this nook and its solid construction. The frank use of beams and posts emphasizes the structural lines and seems particularly appropriate in a farmhouse or rural dwelling. The V-jointed boards of the wainscot, the lintel and recessed shelf of the stone chimneypiece, and

the tiled hearth, are all pleasant features, and the three panels which form the end of the seat serve to shield it from possible draft and at the same time add to the privacy of the inglenook. The Craftsman lantern, a glimpse of which is shown suspended from the ceiling, suggests other possibilities in decorative fittings for the various rooms.

In the recess in the living room there is a built-in seat and double glass doors flanked by casement windows open onto the porch, which is edged with flower-boxes placed between the cement pillars supporting the sloping roof.

On one side of the living-room fireplace is the door of a wood closet which can also be reached from the pantry in the rear. This pantry, which is fitted with an ice-box and a long cupboard, serves as a passageway between the dining room and the kitchen. Steps lead up from the kitchen to the staircase landing, which is also accessible from the reception hall.

The upper floor, which is divided into three bedrooms with a bathroom in the dormer at the back, is arranged with a view to the greatest possible economy of space, and there is plenty of store room and closet room under the slope of the roof. The sleeping porch in front is sheltered by the parapets and is open to the

RURAL DWELLING WITH COMFORTABLY ARRANGED INTERIOR

FIREPLACE NOOK IN LIVING ROOM OF FARMHOUSE, SHOWING FRANK HANDLING OF BEAMS AND WAINSCOTING.

sky, so that believers in the efficacy of outdoor sleeping will be able to get the full benefit of the breeze without being exposed to the view of passersby. Opening as it does from a bedroom, it can be used even in the severest weather, as all dressing is, of course, done indoors. Flower-boxes similar to those around the lower porch could be placed along the edges of the parapet, and would add a welcome note of color to the house.

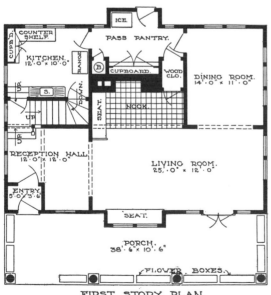

FIRST STORY PLAN.

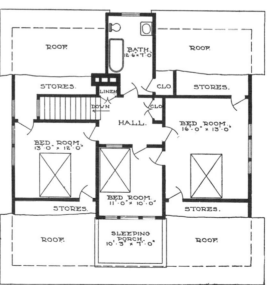

SECOND STORY PLAN.

FARMHOUSE DESIGNED FOR UTILITY AND COMFORT

THIS farmhouse is simple in design and construction, planned to be built entirely of stock material, and the owner can attend to the superintending of the construction, the ordering of the material, etc., without the aid or expense of an architect.

The house is shingled with sawn shingles. This is the most satisfactory of the cheaper materials for exterior walls and can be finished with the ordinary shingle stains. The roof is Ruberoid, battened, and as this roofing is made

an average sized family. The large living room with its broad fireplace will suffice at once as a place for entertainment and the gathering of the family to plan and discuss the work and management of the farm. The opening to the dining room is left wide and a dining porch is provided so that meals may be served in the open.

The laundry tubs have been placed in the summer kitchen—an arrangement which practically takes the work out of the house and at

Published in the Craftsman, February, 1911.
EIGHT-ROOM CRAFTSMAN FARMHOUSE, WITH CONVENIENT SUMMER KITCHEN AND ROOMY PORCHES: NO. 107.

in colors, harmonizing effects can be secured between roof and walls. We specially recommend this roofing material not only because of its cheapness, but because it is practically fireproof—a condition well worth considering in building in the country, where fire protection is often inadequate. With the open construction of the overhanging roof, the hewn log posts for porches and balcony, and the stone foundation, the house will be rustic enough in effect to make the exterior suitable for almost any location in the country.

The interior is planned to meet the needs of

the same time saves the time and labor involved when the laundry is down cellar.

This summer kitchen is one of the delights of the plan, as it provides a place in summer where such tasks as cooking, preserving and canning can be done with much more comfort and under less tiring conditions than in the house. In winter it serves as a convenient place for cooking food for the stock, the cutting-up and preparing of meats, and so forth. Four large bedrooms, bath and sewing room are provided on the second floor. There are plenty of closets and the bedrooms are well

FARMHOUSE DESIGNED FOR UTILITY AND COMFORT

ONE CORNER OF LIVING ROOM IN FARMHOUSE NO. 107: THE CRAFTSMAN FIREPLACE-FURNACE AND THE STAIR-CASE ARE INTERESTING FEATURES OF THIS COMMODIOUS AND SIMPLY ARRANGED INTERIOR.

lighted, having double-hung windows on two sides. A door from the sewing room opens onto the long sleeping porch at the rear, which is sheltered by an extension of the roof. This porch may be edged with flower-boxes, which will serve somewhat as a screen and add a welcome note to the exterior. Vines may also be trained about the pillars of the front and dining porches.

The house may be heated and ventilated by using the Craftsman fireplace-furnace shown in the view of the interior. This will serve for all the rooms, the arrangement of the pipes for the upper rooms being indicated by dotted lines in the floor plan of the second story.

Some idea of the general appearance of the interior and the treatment of woodwork and wall spaces, is given by the illustration above.

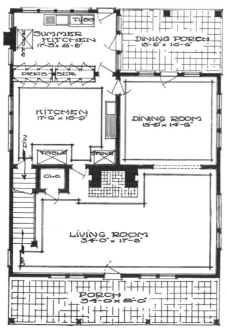

FARMHOUSE NO. 107: FIRST FLOOR PLAN.

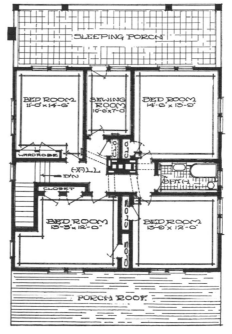

FARMHOUSE NO. 107: SECOND FLOOR PLAN.

COMFORTABLE, CONVENIENT, HOMELIKE FARM-HOUSE WITH CONNECTED WOODSHED AND BARN

Published in The Craftsman, February, 1911.

FARMHOUSE WITH WOODSHED AND BARN: NO. 108.

BUILT on a stone foundation, with walls of sawn shingles, with roof of Ruberoid, and hewn log posts supporting the roofs of pergola, porches and balcony, this farmhouse presents a simple but attractive exterior. The building is planned especially for convenience and economy of labor, and is heated and ventilated by a Craftsman fireplace-furnace. Coal and wood closets are provided where fuel can be stored, easily accessible to fireplace and kitchen. A summer kitchen is also provided containing stove and laundry tubs, while an outdoor dining room, its long table and benches enclosed from the yard by a curved hedge, forms a most charming place for serving meals during the summer.

ONE SIDE OF LIVING ROOM IN FARMHOUSE NO. 108, SHOWING RECESSED FIREPLACE AND EFFECTIVE SIMPLICITY OF WALL TREATMENT.

FARMHOUSE WITH CONNECTED WOODSHED AND BARN

The woodshed provides a passage under shelter to the barn and sufficiently isolates the barn from the house to remove any objectionable features. The barn is not intended to accommodate much stock, but a box stall and one single stall have been planned for horses, and a separate room large enough for three or four cows has been partitioned off with a solid wall. This stall has an outside entrance.

We located the feed bins in the loft and convey the feed to the first floor through metal chutes. A hay chute is also provided. Ample room for carriage, wagon and farm tools is arranged for on the first floor. The corn crib is constructed of slats as shown; this should be lined on all sides, top and bottom, with a fine mesh wire to keep out rats or mice.

One of the great advantages of the fireplace-furnace being located on the first floor is the fact that there is no heat in the cellar. Fruit and vegetables can be stored in the cellar and will keep nicely all the winter.

The second floor plan shows a very simple arrangement. There are four bedrooms of convenient size, and a bathroom, all opening out of the small central hall. Plenty of closets are provided. The two bedrooms at the right have glass doors lead-

ing to the sleeping porch which runs across the side of the house and is sheltered by the roof extension.

The illustration of the living room suggests a simple but interesting treatment of woodwork and walls, and the use of small panes in the windows always adds a decorative note to the interior. The recessed hearth is a somewhat unusual feature, and increases the homelike air of the long cheerful room.

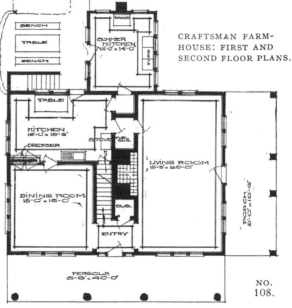

CRAFTSMAN FARMHOUSE: FIRST AND SECOND FLOOR PLANS.

NO. 108.

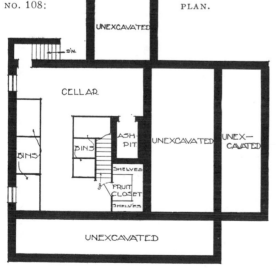

FARMHOUSE NO. 108: CELLAR PLAN.

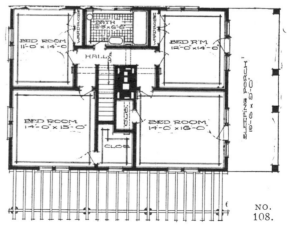

NO. 108.

121

COMPACTLY BUILT CRAFTSMAN FARMHOUSE

Published in The Craftsman, January, 1909.

SIX-ROOM SHINGLED FARMHOUSE, NO. 59.

THE plan of this building is so arranged as to simplify greatly the work of the household and to give a great deal of room within a comparatively small space.

The design is definitely that of a farmhouse, and in this frank expression of its character and use lies the chief charm of the dwelling. The walls are covered with shingles or clapboards, according to the taste or means of the owner. If the beauty of the building were more to be considered than the expense of construction, we should recommend the use of rived cypress shingles. But the ordinary sawn shingle oiled and left to weather, or stained to some unobtrusive tone of green or brown, would give a very good effect.

The roof, of course, would be shingled, and for the sake of durability would be painted rather than stained. As the construction of the house in front is such that a veranda would be rather a disfigurement than an improvement, we have supplied its place by a terrace covered with a pergola. The terrace, of course, would be of cement or vitrified brick, and the construction of the pergola would naturally be rustic in character, especially in the case of a shingled house. One great advantage of the pergola is that the vines which cover it afford sufficient shade in summer, while in winter there is nothing to interfere with the air and sunlight which should be ad-

mitted as freely as possible to the house. We have allowed the roof to come down in an unbroken sweep toward the back because of the

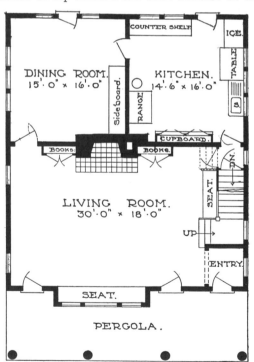

FARMHOUSE NO. 59: FIRST FLOOR PLAN.

COMPACTLY BUILT CRAFTSMAN FARMHOUSE

beauty and uniqueness of it. By this device there is considerable space for storage left over the kitchen and dining room.

The entry opens into the living room. The big chimney being in the middle of the house, the fireplace in the living room is connected with it on one side and with the kitchen range on the other. The fireplace has a bookcase built in on either side, and these bookcases with the two built-in seats form the nucleus of the furnishings.

The dining room is separated from the living room by a door of the usual width. A built-in sideboard is the chief piece of furniture in this room, and a door communicates directly with the kitchen, where there is every convenience combined with the greatest economy of space.

On the second story the arrangement is as convenient and economical as it is below. The upper hall, that communicates with all three of the bedrooms, bathroom and the storage place under the roof, is made small so that all the space possible may be utilized for the rooms. The big sweep of the roof at the back affords a large place for storage, though the walls are not high enough to permit of its being used for any other purpose.

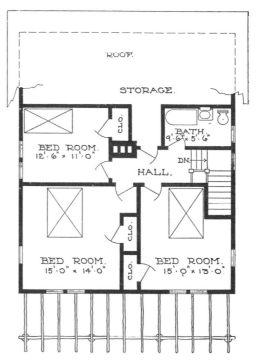

FARMHOUSE NO. 59: SECOND FLOOR PLAN.

REAR VIEW OF CRAFTSMAN SIX-ROOM SHINGLED FARMHOUSE NO. 59.

123

PRACTICAL, INEXPENSIVE ONE-STORY BUNGALOW

THIS small bungalow is a characteristic Craftsman home. We would use split cypress shingles for the walls and split field stone for the foundation. A broad terrace, open to the sky, takes the place of a veranda in front, and the vestibule projects upon this terrace. The roof, which has a very wide overhang, is made of Ruberoid battened at the joints, and its line is broken by the broad low dormer with its group of casement windows—a feature that adds greatly to the structural interest of the building.

The small vestibule, which has a seat on one side and a coat closet on the other, is lighted by casements set high in the wall and also by the lights in the upper part of the door. The framing of door and windows is unusual and very effective, as it brings out the whole front of the vestibule into one structural group. This vestibule opens into a small passageway from which a door on one side leads to a den shut off from the rest of the house, and an open doorway on the other side communicates with the living room. The arrangement of living room and dining room is spacious and open, while the fireplace occupies a deep recess in the living room. The latter, as shown, is wainscoted to the height of the frieze, and the windows and door openings are so placed that the line around the room is unbroken. The top of the wainscot is finished with a square beam instead of a plate rail, and the partition between dining room and living room is indicated by post and panel construction. There is only one group of windows in the living room, but that is so large that almost the entire front wall appears to be of glass.

In the dining room the walls are wainscoted clear to the ceiling, and a group of windows similar to that in the living room gives plenty of light and a pleasant sense of airiness. The combined sideboard and china closets built in below a row of casement windows occupy the whole end of the room. The china closets extend to the ceiling, and the sideboard, which is fifteen feet long, projects several inches beyond the closets.

All the rooms are on one floor, the two bedrooms and a good-sized bathroom occupying the greater part of the space at the rear of the house. The kitchen is small but well equipped, and a large pantry adds greatly to the convenience of the housekeeping arrangements.

There is a closet in each bedroom as well as

Published in The Craftsman, August, 1910.

SIX-ROOM SHINGLED BUNGALOW: NO. 96.

PRACTICAL, INEXPENSIVE ONE-STORY BUNGALOW

PART OF LIVING ROOM OF BUNGALOW NO. 96, WITH VIEW OF DINING ROOM AND BUILT-IN FITTINGS.

in the den, and a good-sized linen closet in the hall. The stairs lead up from the hall to the attic which may be used for storage purposes, and which is lighted by two small windows in each gable and a row of four windows in the low dormer in front. From the pantry stairs lead down to the cellar.

The arrangement of the rooms of this bungalow will be found especially convenient, both for economy of housework and the convenience and privacy of the various members of the household. The sleeping apartments are kept quite separate from the service part of the house and from the living and dining rooms, and while the latter are open and hospitable, serving as a place for the gathering of family and guests, the smaller den provides opportunity for privacy when desired.

All the rooms are of convenient size and are well lighted, the small panes of the casement windows adding to the interest of the exterior as well as of the rooms within, as shown by the illustration of the liv-

ing and dining rooms given above. This view also shows the treatment of the woodwork, the boarded wainscot, the open arrangement of the post and panel construction between the rooms, and the effect of the built-in fittings.

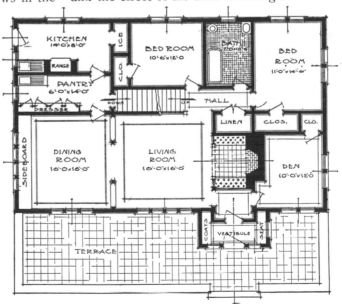

FLOOR PLAN OF SHINGLED BUNGALOW: NO. 96.

125

SEVEN-ROOM SHINGLED CRAFTSMAN COTTAGE

Published in The Craftsman, January, 1912.

SEVEN-ROOM SHINGLED COTTAGE: NO. 127

SHINGLES are used for the walls and roof of this cottage. Pillars of hewn logs are used to support the roof where it slopes over the porch. The windows are all double-hung, with a single lower pane and small panes above. The grouping of these windows, the long lines of the roof and the dormer which breaks it give interest to the exterior of this unpretentious and homelike little dwelling.

Both the dining room and the large living room have fireplaces, and if Craftsman fireplace-furnaces are used they will heat and ventilate the whole house. The effective treatment of the long wall of the living room, with its built-in seat and bookcases, is shown in a perspective view. Kitchen, pantry and a large

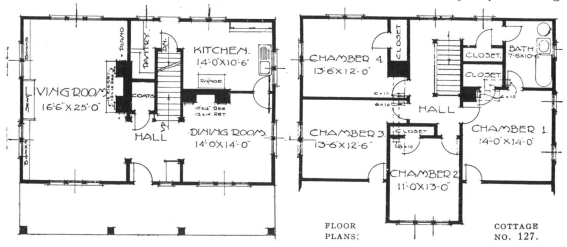

FLOOR PLANS:

COTTAGE NO. 127.

SEVEN-ROOM SHINGLED CRAFTSMAN COTTAGE

FIREPLACE CORNER OF DINING ROOM IN COTTAGE NO. 127, SHOWING CRAFTSMAN FITTINGS AND FURNITURE.

coat closet occupy the remainder of the lower floor plan. Upstairs there are four bedrooms and bath, opening out of the hall which is lighted by three windows in the rear. There are several interior closets as well as storage space beneath the slope of the front roof. The compactness of the rooms of the cottage will make the household work very light.

SIDE OF LIVING ROOM IN COTTAGE NO. 127: A NOTABLE EXAMPLE OF USEFUL AND DECORATIVE WALL TREATMENT

SHINGLED COTTAGE WITH RECESSED PORCHES

Published in The Craftsman, January, 1912.

CRAFTSMAN SHINGLED COTTAGE: NO. 128.

BRICK is used for the foundation and chimney of this cottage and the walls and roof are shingled. The windows are double-hung, small square panes being used in the upper portion. It will be noticed that where the windows are not sheltered by the porch recess or by the overhanging roof they are hooded at the top by springing outward a row of shingles to protect them from storms. These window groups, the recessed corner porch and the trelliswork over the front wall are pleasant features of the exterior; and the vines trained over the trellis, up the corner pillar of the porch, against the chimney at the side, and the small shrubs planted along the base of the walls, all help to knit the little cottage more closely to its surroundings and at the same time break up the straight lines of the building.

The entrance door opens directly into the living room, which is a long and spacious apartment with windows on three sides and a

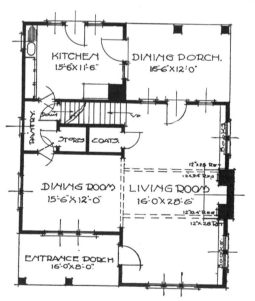

COTTAGE NO. 128: FIRST FLOOR PLAN

SHINGLED COTTAGE WITH RECESSED CORNER PORCHES

door opening onto the corner dining porch at the rear. In the center of the side wall is a Craftsman fireplace-furnace which serves to heat and ventilate the whole cottage. The chimneypiece is of Tapestry brick, and low built-in bookcases fill the wall space on either side. A wide opening leads from the living room into the dining room, which is practically a recess in the larger room, and swing doors through the pantry give access to the kitchen which also opens onto the dining porch. The stairs lead up from one corner of the living room, with a coat closet at the side.

The interior view given here shows the effective handling of the woodwork of the living room, which is merely a natural use of structural parts such as door and window frames, posts, beams, etc. In front of the fireplace we have shown a long Craftsman settle with a table placed behind so that the lamplight will fall over the shoulder of anyone reading. A few pieces of willow furniture such as the armchair shown here will form a pleasant contrast to the oak furniture and add a lighter decorative note to the room.

Three good-sized bedrooms and bathroom are provided on the second floor, each opening out of the narrow L-shaped hall which leads down to the pleasant stair landing. This is

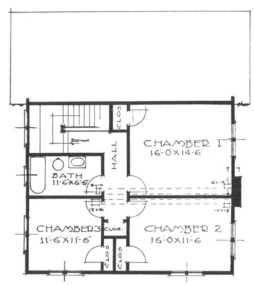

COTTAGE NO. 128: SECOND FLOOR PLAN.

lighted by two windows beneath which a long seat is built. Each bedroom has a closet and there is also a linen closet in the hall.

Although small, the cottage is one which lends itself to interesting furnishing, and with a little thoughtful planning of arrangement and color schemes can be made very homelike.

ONE CORNER OF LIVING ROOM IN COTTAGE NO. 128. THE CRAFTSMAN FIREPLACE-FURNACE OF TAPESTRY BRICK, THE LOW BOOKCASES ON EITHER SIDE, THE PLEASANT WINDOW GROUPS AND THE ARRANGEMENT OF CRAFTSMAN FURNITURE, MAKE THIS ROOM BOTH PRACTICAL AND HOMELIKE.

SMALL SHINGLED HOUSE WITH RIGHT USE OF STRUCTURAL FEATURES AND WOODWORK

WE have suggested the use of shingles for the walls of this simple little cottage because they seem the best adapted to the details of its construction. They should, however, be laid in double course, the top ones being well exposed and the under ones showing not much more than an inch below, giving an interesting effect of irregularity to the wall surface. All the lines of the framework are simple to a degree, but the plainness is relieved by the widely overhanging eaves and rafters of the roof, the well-proportioned

As the floor plans show, the arrangement of the interior is very convenient, the rooms being light and airy and fairly large, and the communication between them as simple as possible to facilitate the work of housekeeping. The entrance door leads directly into the living room, and the first thing one would see on entering would be the fireplace, which is built diagonally across the corner with a built-in seat between it and the landing of the staircase. This fireplace is made of rough red brick, with a wood mantelshelf set on a line

Published in The Craftsman, February, 1907.

SEVEN-ROOM SHINGLED HOUSE: NO. 46.

porch which is balanced by the extension at the rear, the heavy beams which run entirely around the walls and the effective grouping of the windows.

The roof of the porch projects two and a half feet, affording protection even in a driving storm. Also for protection all the exposed windows are capped by small shingled hoods. The eaves of the main roof project over the front for two and a half feet, and the weight is supported by purlins placed at the peak of the roof and at its connection with each of the side walls. This widely projecting roof gives a comfortable and homelike effect of shelter, an effect which is heightened by the way in which the little casement windows on the second story seem to hide under its wing.

with the wainscot. Three steps lead up to the small square landing from which the stairs go up to the second story. Bookcases are placed beneath the window in the opposite corner of the room.

The posts and panels of the wainscoted walls and the fireside seat, and the slight alcove effect of the front group of door and windows with their small square panes, make the room one of much structural interest. The hanging of Craftsman bracket lanterns from the posts above the seat, as shown in the illustration, suggests other possibilities for a useful and decorative arrangement of the various fittings and furnishings of the room.

An attractive feature of the dining room is the little recess in the back with its built-in china closet. Swing doors lead through the

COMPACT SEVEN-ROOM SHINGLED HOUSE

VIEW IN LIVING ROOM OF HOUSE NO. 46, SHOWING CORNER HEARTH, BUILT-IN SEAT AND LOWER END OF STAIRWAY.

pantry, with its ice-box and cupboards, into the kitchen, which communicates with a small entry in the rear.

Upstairs there are three bedrooms and a bathroom. The two front rooms have square closets and in the back bedroom and the hall corner closets are provided.

If greater privacy were wanted downstairs, an ordinary partition and door might be used between dining room and living room instead of the post and panel construction. And if a fireplace nook were desired, the chimneypiece might be placed along the side wall at the left with the seat at right angles to the wall. This would form a comfortable little inglenook, and at the same time the high back of the seat would shield those about the hearth from any draft from the front door.

HOUSE NO. 46: FIRST FLOOR PLAN.

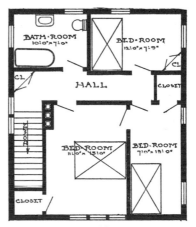

HOUSE NO. 46: SECOND FLOOR PLAN.

RUSTIC BUNGALOW WITH OPEN UPPER STORY

AS this dwelling is to be occupied for only a few weeks of the year, the most rigid economies must be observed in its construction, so that the first cost is not prohibitive and that the investment does not become a burden. The house is therefore planned to be built of stock material, such as can be purchased in any locality, and the simplest methods of construction are recommended. The exterior is of wood with Ruberoid roof, battened.

The plan is shown without foundation. In selecting a site for this bungalow care should be taken to secure a dry, well-drained surface, so that dampness will not rot the floor timbers, as the sills are to rest directly on posts

most delightfully to decoration in cool tones of a gray or green stain.

An abundance of windows have been provided for light and ventilation. Casements are used, being the least expensive to install, as well as giving the added charm of windows which can be thrown wide open. The broad entrance porch, with its balcony overhead, supported by hewn trees for posts, is most pleasing in effect. A living room, three bedrooms and a kitchen are provided on the first floor. No bath is shown because in a summer cottage running water is seldom available, the locality chosen being generally one where public bathing may be had in lake or surf. If,

Published in The Craftsman, March, 1911.   CRAFTSMAN SHINGLED BUNGALOW: NO. 109.

sunk in the ground. A large flat stone will form a good footing for the posts and will prevent the house from settling. Sawn shingles of cedar or cypress may be used for the exterior and may be left to weather. But for a few dollars the owner can himself add much to the beauty as well as to the life of the cottage by applying oil stain to the shingles, selecting harmonizing colors to blend with the colors of the roofing and the surrounding landscape.

The walls are constructed of 3 x 4 dressed spruce or hemlock studs, placed about five feet apart, and over these are nailed North Carolina sheathing boards with the dressed side exposed in the rooms. The overhead beams are left exposed, with the floor above forming the ceiling. This panel construction of side walls and ceiling is at once inexpensive and interesting; the whole interior being of wood, lends itself

however, the owner desires to go to that expense, another partition may be added and a bath placed between two of the bedrooms.

The fireplace, built of stone or brick, laid up with wide joints, will add to the rustic appearance of the interior and afford much comfort to those who have the leisure to spend a few weeks of the early fall in such a pleasant place. A door opens directly from the kitchen to the porch, so that meals may be served in the open.

Ample storage room is provided in the attic by partitioning off the spaces under the eaves to a height of about five feet. Both ends of the attic are left entirely open, and this space will accommodate a number of cots and form most delightful sleeping quarters.

This type of construction, with its provision for open air sleeping, is especially wel-

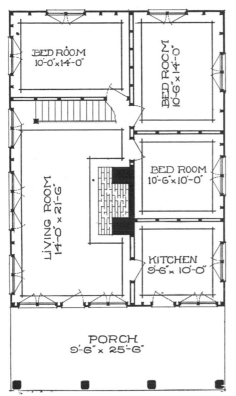

BUNGALOW NO. 109: FIRST FLOOR PLAN.

BUNGALOW NO. 109: SECOND FLOOR PLAN.

come now that people are coming more and more to realize the importance of healthful environment during sleeping as well as waking hours. Medical science has discovered that plenty of fresh air is one of the greatest preventives as well as cures for tuberculosis and many other diseases, and surely those of us who are in good health should welcome equally an opportunity to breathe the purest air during every one of the twenty-four hours. For tuberculosis patients or people at all liable to consumptive developments such a home as the one illustrated here would afford ample chance for the fresh air sleeping which has proved so efficacious.

In addition to the artistic possibilities of its interior this bungalow could be made very attractive outside, with rustic seats on the porch or at the side of the building. A rustic gateway like the one shown here would be a charming feature if the garden boundaries were defined. By using local materials but little expense would be involved, while the pleasure of such picturesque and friendly surroundings would quite compensate for the labor. In any garden, in fact, rustic structures of this sort add a welcome note, and perhaps if we had more inviting seats and sheltering arbors about our homes we might be tempted oftener to work and play where there are flowers and sunlight and pure air.

SUGGESTION FOR A RUSTIC GATEWAY.

SUMMER BUNGALOW WITH OPEN ATTIC

Published in The Craftsman, March, 1911.   FIVE-ROOM BUNGALOW WITH SLEEPING BALCONIES: NO. 110.

THIS little summer cottage has the same general construction as No. 109, previously described. The exterior walls, however, are sheathed and battened, with gables shingled. Rough boards for these outside walls, undressed rafters, hewn posts and stone foundation combine to give enough of the rustic effect to make this house especially suited for a mountain camp. The living room being open to the rafters affords a delightful expanse of spacious walls and ceiling. The balcony is reached by a stairway from kitchen or porch, and the ends of the attic are thrown wide open for air, with the balcony extended out some four feet beyond the outside walls.

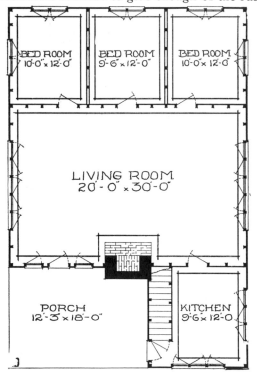

BUNGALOW NO. 110: FIRST FLOOR PLAN.

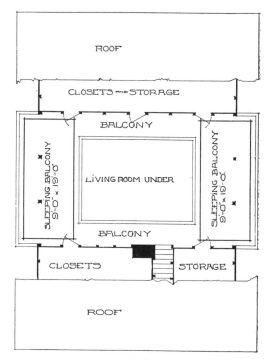

BUNGALOW NO. 110: SECOND FLOOR PLAN.

134

RUSTIC ONE-STORY BUNGALOW, WITH COMPACT INTERIOR AND COMFORTABLE FITTINGS

CONSTRUCTED entirely of dressed lumber, with rough stone for the foundation and chimney, with hewn posts, shingled walls and boarded gables, this bungalow has sufficient of the rustic character to harmonize with its surroundings of woods and mountain.

Casement windows are used, with small panes, and where the windows are not sufficiently sheltered by the roof they are hooded at the top by springing out a row of shingles. Upon the grouping of the windows depends much of the attraction of this very simple exterior.

more definite idea of the homelike effect of the open hearth and inviting fireside seats. The high wainscot, the paneled doors with the square lights in the upper portion, and the simple yet decorative construction of the seats, all are typical of a Craftsman interior. The details, of course, could be modified to suit the taste or convenience of the owner. For instance, the back of the seat on the left of the inglenook could be extended all the way up to the ceiling, if preferred, instead of only part way as shown in the sketch, or a curtain could be hung in the open space to shield those

Published in The Craftsman, May, 1911.

SIX-ROOM SHINGLED BUNGALOW: NO. 116

On entering the living room, the open shelves of books, the fireplace nook with comfortable cushioned seats, and the china closet and wide sideboard in the dining room present an interesting picture. The large groups of casement windows in the front wall and the group over the sideboard will flood the rooms with light and air. The general effect is one large commodious room with so much of the furniture built in that only a table and a few chairs are necessary to complete the furnishing.

The illustration on the next page shows the inglenook in the living room and gives one a

about the hearth from any possible draft and secure a greater sense of privacy. The color and design of the curtain would of course be chosen to harmonize with the cushions and other fittings of the nook, and carry out the general decorative scheme of the rooms. A copper bowl placed in the recess above the mantelshelf would be another welcome glint of color, and sconces could be fitted to the walls as shown in the drawing, or hanging lanterns suspended from the beam which runs across the nook. In fact, the task of furnishing and decorating the rooms will prove full of pleas-

RUSTIC BUNGALOW WITH COMFORTABLE INTERIOR

INGLENOOK WITH STONE CHIMNEYPIECE AND FIRESIDE SEATS IN LIVING ROOM OF RUSTIC BUNGALOW, NO. 116.

ant possibilities for those who take delight in making a home beautiful.

Especially interesting is the arrangement of bedrooms and bath, and the little hall is cur-

tained off from the living room by portières to insure more privacy. A door leading from the kitchen affords communication to the bedrooms without having to go through the dining and living rooms. The kitchen is well arranged with ample pantry and closet room and a small service porch. The pantry has swing doors between dining room and kitchen, and has ample shelf room, one of the shelves being hinged to afford more room when not in use. The kitchen has the usual dresser and a closet, and there is plenty of closet or wardrobe space in each of the bedrooms. A coat closet is also provided in the hall.

The floor plan could of course be modified in various ways to meet special requirements. For example, if two bedrooms were sufficient, the front bedroom could be used as a library or den, and made to open out of the living room instead of the hall. Or the partition might be omitted and the space included in the main room, in which case the bookshelves could be built elsewhere.

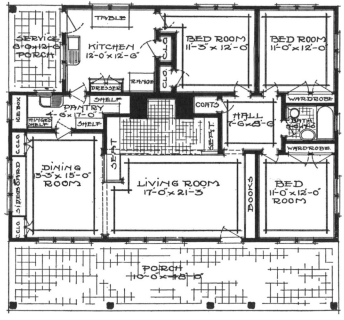

FLOOR PLAN OF RUSTIC BUNGALOW. NO. 116.

136

ONE-STORY SHINGLED CRAFTSMAN BUNGALOW FOR RURAL SURROUNDINGS

Published in
The Craftsman
November, 1908.

SHINGLED
BUNGALOW:
NO. 54.

THIS bungalow is intended for summer although it can be heated sufficiently for winter use if desired. The design is very simple and inexpensive. Shingles are used for the walls. The entrance is at the end, where a little recessed porch floored with red cement extends the whole width of the house. The weight of the gable is supported by four heavy log pillars. The foundation and chimney are of field stone and the floor is kept as near to the level of the ground as possible. An excavation of two feet clear is left under the building, but the exterior effect that is sought is that of the closest possible relation between the house and ground; therefore, from the porch one steps directly off onto the grass.

The interior arrangement is simple and compact, the stone fireplace being in the center. The living room is spacious and homelike, with ample cupboards, and with box couches which add materially to the sleeping accommodations. The kitchen is fitted with cupboards and drawers, and a long closet in the bedroom will be found useful.

Plenty of windows are provided so that the rooms are all light and airy. In fact the little cabin could be made both comfortable and picturesque, while the compactness of its arrangement and practical placing of the built-in furnishings would make the housework light, allowing ample time for outdoor life.

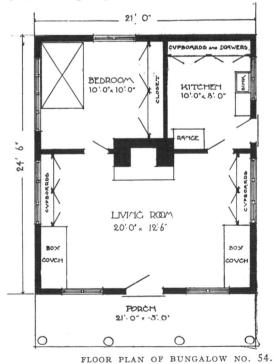

FLOOR PLAN OF BUNGALOW NO. 54.

TEN-ROOM HOUSE FOR TOWN OR COUNTRY LIFE

Published in The Craftsman, July, 1909.

TEN-ROOM HOUSE OF BOARDS AND SHINGLES: NO. 70.

THIS house is built on a foundation of field stone. The lower walls are covered with weather-boarding, and above this rived shingles are used, with vertical boards in the gable. The large living porch is at the side of the house, with glass doors opening from the dining room. It has a low parapet of stone, pillars of wood, floor of cement, and flower-boxes between the posts. The roof of the small entrance porch is also supported by wooden pillars, and wooden seats are built along the sides.

The entrance door leads through a small vestibule into a hall, the end of which is raised to form a landing from which the staircase goes up to the second story. A coat closet fills the space under the stairs.

On one side of the hall a wide opening leads to the living room with its open fireplace and wide built-in seats on each side, with case-ment windows above. The opposite corners of the room are filled with bookshelves, making a very symmetrical arrangement and giving the room a homelike appearance even before

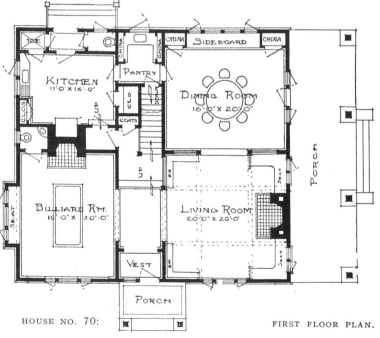

HOUSE NO. 70:

FIRST FLOOR PLAN.

138

TEN-ROOM HOUSE FOR TOWN OR COUNTRY LIFE

the rest of the furnishings have been moved in. Between the living room and dining room is a narrow partition of spindles. The entire end of the dining room is filled with a long built-in sideboard with casement windows set in the wall above, and china closets on each side. A door on the left leads to the pantry, which is fitted with shelves and sink and communicates with the kitchen. A door from the kitchen leads to the stair landing and thus gives ready access to the front door.

The billiard room is large and well lighted, and is fitted with a long window seat, an open fireplace and a small lavatory.

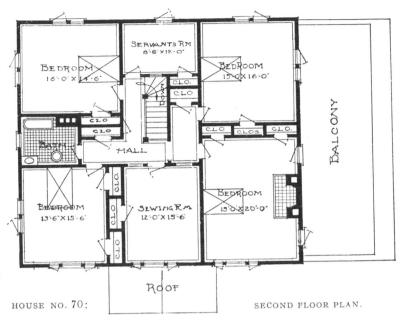

HOUSE NO. 70:   SECOND FLOOR PLAN.

CORNER OF DINING ROOM IN HOUSE NO. 70, WITH BUILT-IN SIDEBOARD AND CLOSETS, AND CASEMENT WINDOWS.

139

COMPACT TWO-STORY CRAFTSMAN HOUSE PLANNED FOR SLOPING SITE

Published in The Craftsman, September, 1910.

NINE-ROOM CRAFTSMAN HOUSE: NO. 98.

ALTHOUGH planned to fit a special site, this house would look equally well in any commanding position. The ground on which it is built includes two lots, the front one low and level and the second one rising in a curve. The rough stone parapet, with its massive irregular coping stones, rises several feet from the lawn below, affording ample room for a line of casement windows that give light to the billiard room which occupies the front of the basement.

On the walls the usual proportions of the clapboards and shingles are reversed, the clapboards being carried much higher than ordinary in order to emphasize the broad effect of the building. The grouping of the windows and the low pitch of the roof tend to increase this effect. From the pergola porch in front a recessed door leads directly into the large living hall. The sheltered position of the door makes a vestibule unnecessary. On each side is a convenient closet in which coats, overshoes, etc., may be kept. On entering, one is greeted at once by the hospitable welcome of the open fireplace with its wide tiled hearth, which occu-

pies the back of the hall. This fireplace really serves for dining and living room as well, for the divisions between the three rooms are so slight that the effect is practically that of one long, spacious apartment. The side wall of the living room on the right is filled by a window seat with built-in bookcases on each side of it. The front and rear walls of this room are broken by window groups, including a glass

door leading out onto the corner porch at the back of the house. The dining room on the opposite side

ROUND DROP-LEAF TABLE FROM THE CRAFTSMAN WORKSHOPS WHICH WOULD FORM A PRACTICAL PART OF THE FURNISHINGS OF ANY HOUSE.

of the hall has its side wall filled by a built-in sideboard flanked by china closets, so that both ends of the long open apartment are full of interest, and form a very practical as well as decorative part of the furnishings. From the dining room a swing door leads into the kitchen, which is fitted with all the necessary conveniences.

At the back of the square living hall is the landing of the staircase which runs up behind the chimneypiece to another landing, which also communicates with the kitchen stairs and from which the main staircase goes on up to the second story. The floor plans give a clear idea of the compactness with which the rooms are arranged and the sense of wide

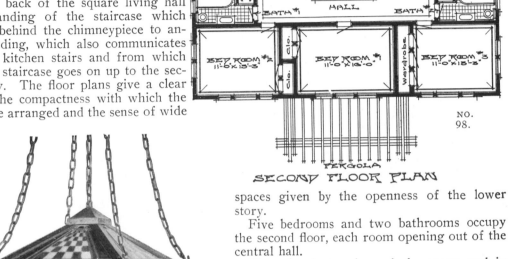

CRAFTSMAN HOUSE:

NO. 98.

SECOND FLOOR PLAN

spaces given by the openness of the lower story.

Five bedrooms and two bathrooms occupy the second floor, each room opening out of the central hall.

There is plenty of wardrobe space, and in one of the rear bedrooms a window seat is built into the recess formed by the corner closet and the wall of the kitchen staircase.

The illustrations of fittings from the Craftsman workshops shown on these pages are merely suggestions of the sort of furnishings which will be found most appropriate for this interior. They are simple in line, solid in construction, and the materials and workmanship that go into the making of them give them a certain dignity and beauty —qualities which must always belong to the ideal home.

DOME OF COPPER OR BRASS, WITH AMBER TINTED PANELS OF HAMMERED GLASS, TO BE USED IN LIBRARY OR OVER DINING TABLE.

UMBRELLA STAND OF SIMPLE, PRACTICAL DESIGN: A USEFUL SUGGESTION FOR CITY OR COUNTRY HOUSE.

CRAFTSMAN HOUSE: NO. 98.

FIRST FLOOR PLAN

CRAFTSMAN FARMHOUSE PLANNED FOR COMFORTABLE HOME LIFE

Published in The Craftsman, December, 1908.

SEVEN-ROOM FARMHOUSE WITH OUTSIDE KITCHEN: NO. 57

B ELIEVING that no form of dwelling better repays the thought and care put upon it than the farmhouse, we give here a design for the kind of dwelling that is meant to furnish a pleasant, convenient and comfortable environment for farm life and farm work. This house is low, broad and hospitable looking in its proportions, and simple in design and construction. The walls are sheathed with clapboards and rest on a low foundation of field stone. The low shingled roof, the groups of casement windows and the long dormer add to the charm of the exterior.

The rooms are arranged with a view to making the work of the household as light as possible. The greater part of the lower floor is taken up by the large living room which practically includes the dining room, as the division between them is so slight. The front door opens into an entry or vestibule divided from the living room by a curtain. Provision is made in this entry for hanging up hats and coats and for keeping other outdoor belongings, such as umbrellas and overshoes.

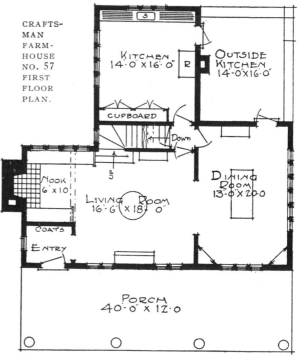

142

FARMHOUSE PLANNED FOR COMFORTABLE HOME LIFE

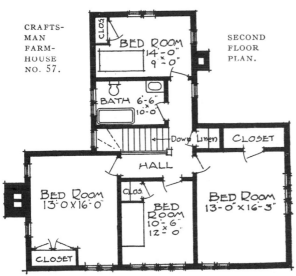

CRAFTS-
MAN
FARM-
HOUSE
NO. 57.

SECOND
FLOOR
PLAN.

The remaining space at this end of the living room is occupied by a fireplace nook. The brick chimneypiece is flush with the wall, and the mantel shelf above is set at the height of the picture rail that runs all around the room, giving an unbroken line, as the tops of the windows, doors and built-in cupboards all conform to it. The built-in seats at either side of the fireplace afford a comfortable lounging place, and the beam that extends across the entrance to the nook gives it a little sense of separation from the rest of the room. The stair landing is lighted with a window of simple design, preferably in amber or hammered antique glass, as either of these give a delightful mellowness to the light.

The kitchen is conveniently arranged with plenty of cupboards, a long window over the sink and unusually wide draining boards which are necessary in a farmhouse kitchen, where large vessels, milk tins and the like have to be washed. Above the draining boards on either side of the sink would be shelves for keeping pots and pans and various cooking utensils. The outside kitchen can be closed in for the winter, as a low wall is built around it and upon this wall could be placed a door, put in where the opening is shown. The laundry and heating apparatus are in the cellar.

Upstairs are four bedrooms. In the front bedroom on the left a window seat could be built in the recess beside the closet. The other rooms are also provided with closets, and shelves are placed in the closet in the hall.

LIVING ROOM IN CRAFTSMAN FARMHOUSE NO. 57, WITH GLIMPSE OF INGLENOOK, ENTRY AND STAIRCASE·

TYPICAL ONE-STORY CRAFTSMAN BUNGALOW SUITABLE FOR EITHER SUMMER OR ALL-YEAR USE

Published in The Craftsman, November, 1908.

ALTHOUGH so arranged that it can be easily heated to the point of comfort in the severest winter weather, this little bungalow is built primarily for a summer home. It is meant to stand in a small clearing made in the natural woodland, and is especially designed for such surroundings. It would be most desirable for those who wish to build an inexpensive summer or week-end bungalow for holiday or vacation use. Of course, the plans would serve perfectly well for a tiny cottage for two or three people to live in, but the design and general character of the building are not adapted to the ordinary town lot, and would be more effective in the country.

Wherever it is possible, local material should be used to give a close relation to the surroundings. Split field stone may be employed for foundation and chimneypiece, and if the site is woodland the thinning out of surrounding trees will furnish logs for the thick hewn pillars that support the porch roof. The unusual size of these pillars and the fact that they are merely peeled logs, hewn here and there to take off the more exaggerated irregularities, does more than any other feature to establish the quaint and "homely" individuality of this little

shelter in the woods. The porch and open-air dining room may be floored with red cement.

The walls are sheathed with boards. An interesting structural decoration is the truss of hewn timber in each gable. This truss projects a foot and a half from the face of the wall and not only gives added support to the roof, but forms a decorative feature that relieves the extreme simplicity of the construction.

The casement windows are all hung so that they will swing outward and are mostly small and set rather high in the wall. At the ends of the building these casements are protected by simple shutters, each made of two wide boards.

The roof may be shingled and colored ac-

FIREPLACE CORNER IN BUNGALOW NO. 53.

144

RUSTIC BUNGALOW FOR SUMMER OR ALL-YEAR USE

THE RECESSED OPEN-AIR DINING ROOM IN CRAFTSMAN COUNTRY BUNGALOW NO. 53: RUSTIC FURNISHINGS.

cording to the character of the location, which has much to do with deciding the color as well as the shape of the roof. One thing it is well to remember, that while a roof may be stained to a green, brown or gray tone, paint should be used if it is to be red, as the effect is much more satisfactory than when a red stain is tried.

Southern pine would be suitable for finishing the interior, and may be stained green or brown to harmonize with the color scheme of the furnishings.

The fireplace may be built of selected split field stone and fitted with a hood like that shown in the detail of the living room.

The interior arrangement is so convenient as to give the utmost space within the small compass. The living room leads into the open-air dining room or porch at the back, which can be left open in summer and glassed in for cold weather. There is plenty of cupboard and closet room, the kitchen being provided with shelves over which are casement windows overlooking the recessed porch. On each side of these shelves are built-in cupboards. A china closet is placed beside the living room fireplace, and small panes are used in its glass doors as in the other doors and windows of the room.

In addition to the living room, kitchen and bathroom, there are two bedrooms which occupy the other side of the plan. If only one bedroom were needed, the space of the front one could be included in the central room.

As suggested in the illustration of the open-air dining room shown above, rustic furnishings would be found very appropriate for this type of dwelling, and would harmonize with the rest of the construction. In fact, rustic furniture could be used not only on the recessed porch, but throughout the interior, if desired, especially if the bungalow were intended only for summer use. If it were used for a permanent all-year home, solid oak pieces would probably be preferred for the rooms, and very simple Craftsman fittings could be chosen, quite in keeping with the general character of the bungalow.

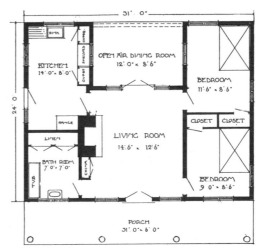

FLOOR PLAN OF BUNGALOW NO. 53.

145

ARCHITECTURAL DEVELOPMENT OF THE LOG CABIN IN AMERICA

WHAT is there about a log cabin that appeals to our imagination, that seems so alluring and full of the suggestion of romance? Is it not because the house of logs is a part of our heredity? It was a primitive home to man, a rudimentary sheltering of domestic life, a place of safety where love and friendship could be shut in and foe and danger shut out. The early homes of our Germanic ancestors were huts in the forest, sometimes built around a central tree which grew up through the roof and spread its sheltering branches over the dwelling. We came from the forest, and trees formed our home and our protection. And so today a house built of wood which has not been metamorphosed into board and shingle, but still bears the semblance of the tree, rouses in us the old instinctive feeling of kinship with the elemental world that is a natural heritage.

To us in America the log cabin seems a near friend. For many of us it was the home of our immediate ancestors, and it forms a vital part of the life of the white man in this continent. What a train of historical reminiscence the mere thought of the log cabin awakens: the landing of the first settlers, the unbroken wilderness of the primeval forests, the clearing of the ground, the building of the first homes. How great must have been the need of the comfort of the hearth and the strength of fellowship in that lonely and desperate struggle against the elements, the foe and starvation! Scattered far over this continent, moving northward, southward and westward, the log cabin has been the pioneer of civilization, the sign of the determination of the white man to face the unknown and to conquer all obstacles. Viewed in this light, it seems of a certain poetic significance that Lincoln, one of the greatest of the nation's leaders, should have been born and reared in a log cabin.

Since the log house has played so important a part in our history its development into a definite and characteristic type of architecture might give us something national, something peculiarly American in suggestiveness. There are elements of intrinsic beauty in the simplicity of a house built on the log cabin idea. First, there is the bare beauty of the logs themselves with their long lines and firm curves. Then there is the open charm of the structural features which are not hidden under plaster and ornament, but are clearly revealed—a charm felt in Japanese architecture, which is, as Cram has said, "the perfect style in wood as Gothic is the perfect style in stone." The Japanese principle, "The wood shall be unadorned to show how beautiful is that of which the house is made," is true of the Craftsman development of the log house. For in most of our modern houses "ornament by its very prodigality becomes cheap and tawdry," and by contrast the quiet rhythmic monotone of the wall of logs fills one with the rustic peace of a secluded nook in the woods.

Of the distinction and charm of such a type the log house at Craftsman Farms is a proof, for it is a log cabin idealized. Some idea of its homelike beauty can be gathered from the views and floor plans given here. And in addition several smaller and simpler forms of this construction are shown—little log bungalows for summer or all-year use, in woods, or mountains, or by the shore.

THE LOG HOUSE BUILT AT CRAFTSMAN FARMS

Published in The Craftsman, November, 1911: Designed and Built by Gustav Stickley.
VIEW OF LOG HOUSE AT CRAFTSMAN FARMS, SHOWING ENCLOSED PORCH, FIFTY-TWO BY FOURTEEN FEET.

AS in the pioneer days, the space for this house had first to be cleared in the forest. The abundant chestnut trees were cut down and of them the house is built. The logs are hewn on two sides and peeled and the hewn sides laid together and chinked with cement mortar. The logs are stained the color of the bark.

A stone foundation runs under the whole building, including the wide veranda across the front of the house. The most practical piece of furniture here is a long combination bench and wood-box in which is kept the smaller wood for the fires.

From the veranda a wide door leads into the great living room with its fireplace at either end. The large hearths, which have special ventilating and heating appliances, are built of field stone gathered on the place and are topped with low-hanging hoods. Most of the available wall space is filled by bookcases. Above the bookcases and over the settles are windows with small diamond panes, and the light is softened to a mellow glow by casement curtains of burnt orange. The color scheme of the whole room reminds one of the forest— brown and green, with the glint of sunshine through the leaves, suggested by the gold of the windows and the gleam of copper in the

hearth-hoods, the door-latches and the vases and bowls on the bookcases and table.

The dining room runs parallel to the living room. Here also is a big ventilating hearth. These fireplaces heat the entire house with hot water and warm air.

Beyond the dining room is the kitchen, a large room, light and airy, painted white, with a large range. There are special appliances for convenience in washing dishes, etc.

The main bedrooms on the second floor are at the two ends of the house; one of them is furnished and decorated in yellow and seems aglow with sunshine; the other, a much larger room, is done in blue and gray with woodwork of dark gumwood. The walls are covered with gray Japanese grass-cloth, the hearth is of dull blue Grueby tiles with a brass hood, and the furniture is gray oak.

The illustrations give but an inadequate idea of the charm and comfort of the interior, its harmony with nature and its unity of the best of civilization with the best in cruder forms of life. Three views are given of the great living room—the first showing the big stone fireplace at one end with bookshelves at the side and Craftsman chairs and table grouped around the hearth. A second view, at the top of page 149, gives one some impression of the

147

THE LOG HOUSE AT CRAFTSMAN FARMS

SIDE VIEW OF LOG HOUSE AT CRAFTSMAN FARMS.

DETAIL IN ONE END OF THE LIVING ROOM, SHOWING CRAFTSMAN FURNITURE ABOUT THE BIG STONE FIREPLACE.

THE LOG HOUSE AT CRAFTSMAN FARMS

VIEW OF GREAT LIVING ROOM, WITH STAIRCASE AT THE LEFT AND STONE CHIMNEY AT THE FURTHER END.

DETAIL OF LIVING ROOM, WITH ENTRANCE INTO THE DINING ROOM: THE LOG CONSTRUCTION IS INTEREST-INGLY SHOWN HERE.

ONE END OF THE DINING ROOM IN THE LOG HOUSE: THE FURNITURE IS FROM THE CRAFTSMAN WORKSHOPS.

SIDE OF DINING ROOM, SHOWING LONG CRAFTSMAN SIDEBOARD: THE LOGS IN THIS ROOM ARE FINISHED WITH A WOOD OIL WHICH GIVES A DELIGHTFUL MELLOW TONE AS THOUGH SUNLIGHT WERE POURING INTO THE ROOM.

THE LOG HOUSE AT CRAFTSMAN FARMS

ONE CORNER OF THE LARGE BEDROOM ON THE SECOND FLOOR OF THE LOG HOUSE, WITH ALCOVE FOR BED.

wide hospitable spaces of the interior, showing the long vista down the room with the other fireplace at the further end, the stair-case on the left and the big glass doors opening onto the veranda at the right. The lower view on the same page shows a detail of the room, including the long table, the piano, and a glimpse through the curtained opening into the dining room beyond. Here again one feels the harmony of the carefully-designed furnishings with the more primitive dignity of the log construction. The remaining views show dining room and one of the bedrooms.

THE LOG HOUSE: FIRST FLOOR PLAN.

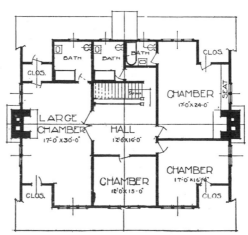

THE LOG HOUSE: SECOND FLOOR PLAN.

LOG COTTAGE FOR SUMMER CAMP OR PERMANENT COUNTRY HOME

Published in The Craftsman, March, 1907.

CRAFTSMAN COTTAGE OF LOGS, WITH STONE FOUNDATION AND CHIMNEY, AND SHINGLED ROOF: THE TWO **LONG** PORCHES AND THE DINING PORCH AT THE REAR GIVE AMPLE ROOM FOR OUTDOOR LIVING: NO. 48.

INTERIOR VIEW IN COTTAGE NO. 48, SHOWING LIVING-ROOM INGLENOOK WITH STONE CHIMNEYPIECE AND **BUILT**-IN CORNER SEATS, AND DINING TABLE IN THE FOREGROUND: THE NATURAL USE OF THE LOGS AND **DECORATIVE** EFFECT RESULTING FROM PRACTICAL HANDLING OF STRUCTURAL FEATURES IS MOST HOMELIKE.

LOG COTTAGE FOR SUMMER CAMP OR PERMANENT HOME

ALTHOUGH this log bungalow is primarily intended for a summer home, it is so carefully planned and so well constructed that it could be used as a regular dwelling all the year round. While the lines of the building are simple to a degree, the proportions and details have all been so thoughtfully considered that with all this simplicity and freedom from pretense there is no suggestion of bareness or crudity. It is essentially a log cabin for woodland life, and looks just that; yet it is a warm, comfortable, roomy building, perfectly drained and ventilated, and if properly built ought to last for many generations.

There is a foundation of stone or cement, sufficiently high to secure good drainage and save the lower logs from decay. This foundation, however, is almost entirely concealed by terracing the soil up to the top of it, to the level of the porch floors. By this means perfect healthfulness is secured, and at the same time the wide, low cottage of logs appears to rest upon the ground in the most primitive way.

The logs used in building have the bark stripped off and are stained to a dull grayish brown that approaches as closely as possible the color of the bark. The removal of the bark prevents rotting, and the stain restores a color that harmonizes with the surroundings.

The wide porches afford plenty of room for outdoor living. One porch is recessed at the end to form a square dining porch, which opens into the kitchen and also into the big room which is a combined living room and indoor dining room.

The entry opening from the porch gives access on one side to the two bedrooms, and on the other leads by a wide opening into the main room. The walls and partitions are of logs and the ceiling is beamed with logs flattened on the upper side to support the floor above. The fireplace, like the chimney outside, is built of split stone, and is in a nook formed or suggested by the two logs placed one above the other across the ceiling logs, and by the two posts at the ends of the fireside seats.

The perspective view of the living room shows what a decorative effect results from this simple rustic treatment, and how entirely the furnish-

ings are in keeping with the purpose and character of the log construction. There is a primitive, picturesque quality about the whole that would be lacking in a more formal interior, and the natural use of the logs seems to relate the rooms very closely to the exterior of the cottage and the woods and hills around.

The upper story may be arranged as the builder pleases. If intended for a permanent home, it can be divided into bedrooms and a bath, but for camp life in the woods a large single room may be left where things can be stored and cots put up or hammocks slung.

The expense of furnishing the bungalow would be somewhat reduced by the built-in fireside seats in the living room and the long seat which stretches beneath the windows in the opposite wall. These could be made with hinged tops, thus providing very useful storage space in addition to the large closet between the living room and bedroom, the kitchen cupboards and the space below the stairs.

If a larger bedroom were desired on the first floor, the entry shown in the plan might be omitted, including this space within the adjacent bedroom and using the door in the corner of the recessed dining porch as the entrance door. Or if only one bedroom were needed a room might be used as library.

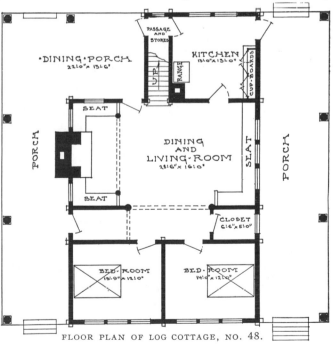

FLOOR PLAN OF LOG COTTAGE, NO. 48.

153

SMALL BUT COMFORTABLE LOG DWELLING

Published in The Craftsman, March, 1907.

LOG HOUSE WITH RUSTIC INTERIOR: NO. 49.

A HILLTOP or slight elevation is the site for which this little cottage was designed, and the ground is terraced to the level of the porch floors, concealing the foundation and seeming to connect the building more closely with the soil. The main roof and that of the porch are shingled, and the columns supporting the latter are thick peeled tree trunks, harmonizing with the peeled and stained logs of the walls. The chimneys are made of split stone. Flower-boxes at the upper windows give a little touch of grace and color that is

LIVING ROOM IN LOG HOUSE NO. 49, WITH UNIQUE CHIMNEYPIECE CONSTRUCTION AND RUSTIC FIRESIDE SEATS

SMALL BUT COMFORTABLE LOG DWELLING

unusually attractive against the brown background of logs. The porch is floored with red cement and the steps leading up to the house are of split stone laid in cement and smoothed off.

The central living room is simple in construction, but there is a dignity in the unbroken lines of the logs that is very effective. An interesting structural feature of the stone chimney-piece is the framing made by the ends of the logs forming the partition on each side of the bathroom, and the log that crosses the mantel-breast at the top, like a lintel. On either side of this fireplace is a large settle built of peeled saplings stained to the same color as the logs of the house. The supports for the seat cushions and the backs are made of ropes twisted and knotted around the frame of the settle. The seat cushions and pillows are of canvas or some such sturdy material in keeping with the rustic interior.

There are two downstairs sleeping rooms, one on each side of the bath. The upper story, which is left undivided, has plenty of light and ventilation, so that it could easily be partitioned into rooms if desired. Casement windows are used throughout, hooded where exposed to the weather. Dutch doors, V-jointed,

RUSTIC PERGOLA FITTED UP FOR OUTDOOR LIVING.

and with large strap hinges, are used for outside doors.

In this sort of cottage, where the porch is likely to be much in use for outdoor meals and as a cool, shady place for work, rest or play, rustic furniture would be as practical as it would be charming. A long seat, a few chairs and a table would serve all the purposes of usefulness and comfort, and would be in perfect harmony with the rest of the building, helping to carry out the rustic effect of the log construction. Or perhaps down by the water's edge or in some other pleasant spot a rustic pergola could be erected, like the one shown above, with vine-clad pillars and roof, inviting chairs, a little table for books or sewing or afternoon tea, and possibly a swinging seat suspended between two of the posts. Thus the hospitality of the log dwelling would be extended as far as possible into the nature world around it, luring one always from the shelter of the cottage into the fresh mountain air, while the unity of the log construction would link the little home more closely to the surrounding woods of which its walls were once a living part. In fact there are various possibilities for practical and picturesque constructions of this sort which ingenuity and skill could devise, at little labor and expense.

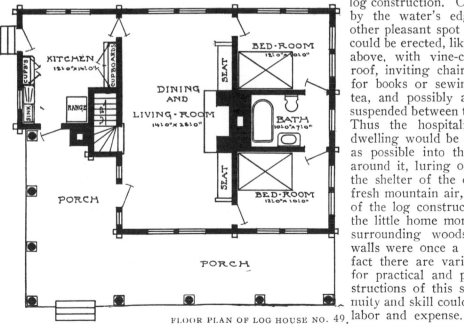

FLOOR PLAN OF LOG HOUSE NO. 49.

LITTLE WOOD COTTAGE ARRANGED FOR SIMPLE COUNTRY LIVING

Published in The Craftsman, March, 1907.

RUSTIC COTTAGE BUILT OF SLABS: NO. 50.

THIS cottage is built of slabs, and while not actually as massive as log construction, gives the same effect of primitive and rugged comfort. The slabs are peeled, nailed to the sheathing of the walls, and stained as nearly as possible to the color of bark. The proportions of the building are low and broad. The widely spreading roof is shingled, the porch columns are logs peeled and stained, and the foundation is concealed under the terrace. The front porch serves all the purposes of an outdoor living room, and the one in the rear is intended for a dining porch, whenever the weather permits.

In the living room every feature of the construction is frankly revealed, and this forms the chief element of decoration. The deep nook that divides the porches is the center of comfort and restfulness for the whole house. Bookshelves are built in on each side of the big fireplace of split stone, and there are two large box-seats made of peeled slabs. The nook has no ceiling, but extends up into a gable, separated by a railing from the attic.

Another fireplace is built in the rear wall of the living room, in this instance the placing of seats being left to the choice of the owner. This end of the room, being between the dining porch and the kitchen, is intended to

be used as an indoor dining room whenever the weather is not mild enough for meals to be carried out onto the porch. The front wall of the living room is filled by a group of three windows, and on the right are doors leading to the two bedrooms, in one of which is a long window seat. The kitchen is provided with ample shelf and storage room, and between the kitchen and bedroom walls the stairs lead up from the living room to the attic. This may be arranged as desired, either divided into several small bedrooms or left in one large room for storage purposes or to

SUGGESTION FOR A RUSTIC GATEWAY AND SEAT.

156

RUSTIC COTTAGE ARRANGED FOR SIMPLE COUNTRY LIVING

INTERIOR VIEW OF COTTAGE NO. 50, SHOWING SPACIOUS LIVING ROOM AND RECESSED FIREPLACE NOOK.

accommodate cots and hammocks when extra sleeping room is required.

The view of the living room and inglenook shown above suggests a satisfactory method of handling the structural features of the interior, the natural use of the woodwork being especially appropriate for this type of building. In fact, the arrangement of the bungalow, and the way in which the structure itself is made the basis of all decorative effect, are both an illustration and suggestion of how much can be accomplished by working along these practical, straightforward lines. While in this instance, of course, the design and scale of the cottage is of the most unpretentious, it embodies in its simple construction many of these characteristics which are typical of the Craftsman ideal home.

Rustic furniture for the porch would be serviceable and in keeping with the slab walls of the building, and the sketch of the rustic gateway, with its pergola roof draped with wistaria and the primitive charm of the little seat below, suggests an appropriate entrance to the garden, and may serve to suggest other vari-

ations on the same theme. A circular rustic seat, for instance, might be built around one of the neighboring trees.

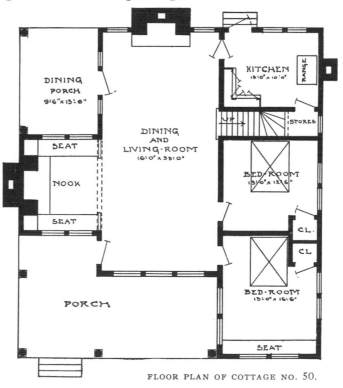

FLOOR PLAN OF COTTAGE NO. 50.

157

COMFORTABLE ONE-STORY BUNGALOW OF LOGS

ROUGH stone foundation, walls of log, and roof of colored Ruberoid are the materials used for this bungalow. The cement floor of the recessed entrance porch is extended beyond the house line as shown, and a log pergola is set on a cement floor at the rear of the building.

The floor plan has been worked out with an idea of economy of effort in housekeeping.

The entrance door opens directly from the porch into the living room, the deep recess sheltering it sufficiently to make a vestibule unnecessary. On either side of the door are two casement windows with small panes. In fact this style of window is used throughout the building, being more suitable for a rural dwelling than the double-hung type, and the small panes breaking up the surface of the walls and adding considerably to the interest of both the exterior of the bungalow and the rooms within.

The center of comfort and charm of the interior is of course the open fireplace which occupies the center of one of the living-room walls and uses the same chimney as the flue of the kitchen range just behind.

A coat closet is conveniently located on one side of the fireplace, while the space on the other has a comfortable built-in seat. The open bookshelves on the other side of the door to the pergola and the groups of high casements break up the wide expanse of wall space and form an interesting group of furnishings.

Both bedrooms are separated from the living room by a narrow hall, and the bath is located between the bedrooms—an arrangement combining convenience and privacy. Ample closet room is provided, and the groups of windows are so situated as to allow cross ventilation.

On the opposite side of the house is the dining room, which, owing to the limitations of the floor plan, is separated from the main room more than is usual in a Craftsman interior. In the present instance, however, this arrangement may be found preferable, as it affords more opportunity for privacy and gives ready access between kitchen, pantry and dining room. Both the kitchen and pantry are arranged with the utmost convenience, with plenty of table and closet room and two sinks and although neither room is large the very compactness of the arrangement makes for economy of housework. The dining room, like the bedroom at the opposite corner, has front and side window groups as well as smaller

Published in The Craftsman, May, 1911.

FIVE-ROOM LOG BUNGALOW: NO. 115.

FIREPLACE CORNER OF LIVING ROOM IN BUNGALOW NO. 115, SHOWING CHIMNEYPIECE OF SPLIT FIELD STONE WITH RECESSED SHELF, AND INTERESTING USE OF WOOD FOR WALLS AND BUILT-IN FIRESIDE SEAT.

casements placed rather high in the wall overlooking the front recessed porch.

The little rear porch built under the main roof adjoining the kitchen may be glassed in winter and screened in summer, and will thus serve as an additional room for kitchen and laundry work.

The interior view given above shows the fireplace corner of the living room and gives a general idea of the appearance of the rest of the interior. The chimneypiece of split field stone, with the deeply recessed shelf, though simple in construction forms a very effective part of the structure, and emphasizes the hospitable air of the spacious room. The corner seat on the left, with its wainscoted back of wide V-jointed boards, could be made very comfortable with a few pillows, and the casement windows in the wall above as well as the small glass panes of the door that leads to the pergola porch at the rear, all help to make the room a pleasant, homelike place.

In this bungalow, as in most of the others shown, a few pieces of rustic furniture grouped about the porch would help to increase its

hospitality and comfort, and would insure the bringing of many little household tasks into the fresh air whenever the weather permitted. Seats could be placed on each side of the front porch beneath the casement windows, and rustic fittings could be used for the rear porch.

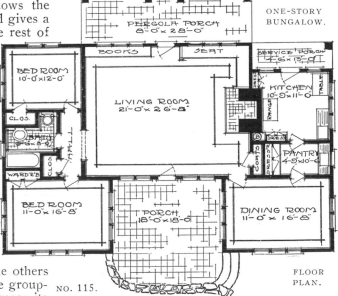

NO. 115.

PERMANENT SUMMER CAMP OF LOGS WITH TOP STORY ARRANGED FOR OUTDOOR SLEEPING

Published in The Craftsman, August, 1911.

PERMANENT SUMMER LOG CAMP: NO. 121.

WE have planned here a log building for a summer camp, so inexpensively and simply built that it can be closed with safety during the winter and easily put into livable order each spring.

The logs are placed upright and chinked with a mixture of one part Portland cement and three parts sand. This is a permanent chinking and will take a stain like the logs if desired. The main room, with fireplace and built-in seat, may be used as the dining room. The windows are casement, which are much cheaper than double-hung windows and can be easily removed and screens inserted for the

VIEW OF LIVING ROOM IN LOG CAMP, NO. 121, SHOWING STONE CHIMNEYPIECE AND BUILT-IN CORNER SEAT.

ventilation of the rooms during the summer.

The main feature is the large open sleeping room upstairs which may be sheltered from wind or rain by duck curtains, and closed up entirely in winter by batten blinds. This sleeping room may be separated into as many small dressing rooms as desired by curtains run on wires or on wooden poles and drawn back when not needed to insure a free circulation of fresh air.

The illustration given here shows the rugged simplicity of the interior, which in spite of its rustic character, holds many possibilities for the making of a comfortable home. The irregular split field stone of the fireplace, with its broad opening and plain

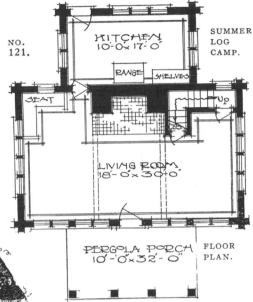

SUGGESTION FOR A RUSTIC GARDEN SEAT.

shelf, the corner seat, the casement windows, with their small, square panes, and the sturdy construction of the logs and boards of walls and ceiling, all combine to form a picturesque background for whatever furnishings may be introduced. Rustic chairs and tables would, of course, harmonize perfectly with this type of construction, but plain oak pieces could be used if preferred, and willow would be both practical and appropriate. On the porch and beneath the trees about the building, rustic seats and benches and small tables would prove a welcome addition to the belongings of the camp, and would extend the boundaries of its comfort

and hospitality. We are showing here sketches of a sheltered seat and arbor, which may serve to suggest other possibilities along the same lines. The putting up of such structures would be a delightful task for the boys of the party, who would no doubt welcome a chance to exert their ingenuity and muscles in such an effective way and prove their skill as builders and carpenters. In fact, a camp of this sort will be found to afford endless opportunities for the development of all those outdoor tasks and pastimes in which labor becomes a source of wholesome joy.

A DECORATIVE GRAPE ARBOR WITH FLOWERS PLANTED FROM POST TO POST

LOG BUNGALOW FOR SUMMER USE, WITH COVERED PORCH AND PARTIALLY OPEN SLEEPING ROOM

Published in The Craftsman, August, 1911.

SUMMER BUNGALOW OF LOGS NO. 122.

VERY like the one previously shown is this camp, both in purpose and general construction. Here, however, the logs are placed horizontally and a long porch is provided, covered, like the main roof, with Ruberoid. The stone fireplace and chimney add to the comfort and picturesqueness of the building, and the upper apartment, being open at both ends, provides an airy place to sleep.

From the porch a door leads into the large living room, and on each side of the door are groups of casement windows with small square panes. Similar windows are also placed in the opposite wall and on each side of the fireplace. In one corner is the staircase leading up to the big, airy room above. A wide opening from the living room leads into the kitchen, which is fitted with long shelves and a stove, and like the living room, has a door opening onto the porch and another door at the rear. A closet is provided in the space beneath the stairs.

The interior view shows one corner of the living room with its stone chimneypiece and massive log construction. The heavy central

PERGOLA PORCH OF SPLIT STONE AND LOGS.

162

PART OF BIG LIVING ROOM IN LOG BUNGALOW NO. 122, SHOWING STONE CHIMNEYPIECE AND CASEMENT WINDOWS, AND EFFECT OF PRIMITIVE COMFORT RESULTING FROM THE WISE USE OF STRUCTURAL FEATURES.

log that runs across the ceiling is in reality two joined in the middle and supported by a post of hewn wood, like the pillars of the porch.

As to the porch itself, pergola construction could be used if preferred, with pillars of split stone, as suggested in the detail sketch, and another porch might be added at the rear of the bungalow if desired. In fact, like all the designs in this book, the plans and the construction may be modified to suit the special requirements of the owner.

The use of vines about the stone chimney and pillars of the porch will add greatly to the charm of the building, and make it even more definitely a part of its surroundings.

In this bungalow, as in the one previously described, box-seats can be built in around the rooms, providing useful storage space for the winter, and rustic chairs and tables, simple and easily made, will prove both an economical and harmonious form of furnishing.

With such a camp, hospitality can be extended indefinitely, for with a living room and kitchen, tent bed-

rooms, hammocks and sleeping bags will afford accommodations for week-end parties.

Since oxygen has proved such an important factor in the prevention and cure of disease, this bungalow, with its open upper story, would be just the thing for a consumptive patient or anyone whose health necessitated the greatest possible amount of fresh air, day and night. Its simplified interior would entail little work, leaving ample time for outdoor life.

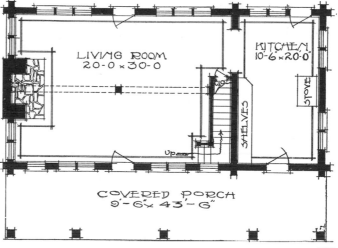

FLOOR PLAN OF LOG BUNGALOW: NO. 122.

CRAFTSMAN COUNTRY SCHOOLHOUSE OF LOGS

Published in The Craftsman, July, 1911.

CRAFTSMAN LOG SCHOOLHOUSE: NO. 119.

THE rural schoolhouse has in many instances grown into the poorest imitation of city educational institutions, in no way suited to the rural life and environment of farm boys and girls. In most cases as it exists today it not only does not fit them to understand, appreciate and make good in farm life, but actually creates a spirit of discontent with country existence and distaste for real work of any sort. This is a disaster not only to the community, but to the nation, to say nothing of the boys and girls.

America must, for progress' sake, have good country schools, suited to rural conditions. We must have townships that are successful without relation to cities, and people who are contented to dwell in the townships. How to bring this about is one of the most important economic questions of the times. It has seemed to us that something toward this end might be accomplished through the right kind of schools—schools that might become, as did the guildhalls of Mediæval times, the center of a widespread general activity and progress. Why make our schoolhouses such dull, uninviting spots that children must be driven into

them and parents never enter? Why not build schools which will develop the community spirit and definitely prepare the pupils for the kind of lives they are most likely to live? The school should suggest that work, if well done, is not drudgery, but one of the greatest factors in the betterment and uplifting of humanity.

Believing that what our country life needs so vitally is better social, economic and educational advantages, we are showing here two schoolhouses, each designed to be of service to every resident of the district where it is built.

The smaller schoolhouse. No. 119, is made of logs dressed on two sides so that they fit together—the inside and outside left round. The chinking is of cement mortar, which is permanent and takes a stain with the logs, if staining is desired.

The direction of the light is from casement windows at the back and left, and the teacher's desk is placed where full view is had of the two cloak rooms, which are provided with lavatories. Bookcases, closets and blackboards are arranged for in the main room. In rural schools all grades must be accommodated in

CORNER IN SCHOOLHOUSE NO. 119, WITH FIREPLACE-FURNACE, BOOKCASES AND BLACKBOARD: THE ARRANGE-
MENT OF STONE IN THE CHIMNEY AND MASSIVE EFFECT OF THE LOGS MAKE THIS AN INTERESTING INTERIOR.

one room, so low tables have been set in a bright corner for the little ones. Desk room is provided for forty-two students, and when lectures are given that interest the community at large the kindergarten table can be removed and extra chairs placed around the room, greatly increasing the seating capacity.

Both schoolhouses are planned to be heated and ventilated with a Craftsman fireplace-

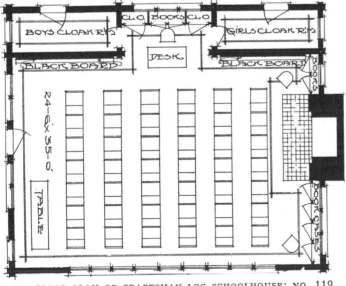

FLOOR PLAN OF CRAFTSMAN LOG SCHOOLHOUSE: NO. 119.

furnace, which is so simple in management that it can be taken care of by the children themselves. A great advantage of such heating is that fire can easily be kept over night so that the schoolroom will be warm in the morning.

The view of the interior shows the corner of the classroom in which the Craftsman fireplace-furnace is built. The recessed shelf and decorative placing of the irregular stones in the chimneypiece, and the massive effect of the logs make the interior very interesting from a structural standpoint, and the arrangement of the built-in bookcases, with their small glass panes, the casement windows, blackboards and closets, should prove practical and convenient.

Both this schoolhouse and the one on the next page are very simple in design, and could be enlarged to meet the special needs of the community. They suggest, however, what may be accomplished along these lines, and if they help to awaken keener interest in the important subject of rural education and to stimulate a desire for more practical, comfortable and beautiful country schools, they will have served their purpose.

RURAL SHINGLED SCHOOLHOUSE PLANNED WITH CONNECTING WORKROOM

Published in The Craftsman, July, 1911.   RURAL SCHOOLHOUSE WITH CONNECTING WORKROOM: NO. 120.

ONE SIDE OF MAIN ROOM IN SCHOOLHOUSE NO. 120, WITH BRICK FIREPLACE-FURNACE AND BUILT-IN BOOKCASES.

RURAL SCHOOLHOUSE WITH CONNECTING WORKROOM

SHINGLES are used for this schoolhouse, for both roof and walls. Inside, the walls and ceiling are finished with plaster. The workroom is separated from the main room by folding doors, which can be thrown open to form a hall where lectures on scientific farming can be given, political meetings held, entertainments of a social nature enjoyed. This workroom is fitted with a fireplace of its own so that it can be used separately if desired. It may serve as a metal or woodworking shop, with the older boys in charge of the younger

FLOOR PLAN OF SHINGLED SCHOOLHOUSE: NO. 120.

ones at times. Or, it can be shut off from the main room while special instruction is given by visiting teachers to the advanced pupils. It can be used by the girls as a sewing room, and there are separate shelves or lockers on either side of the fireplace to hold the various materials which the children will require for their work.

Ample blackboard space is provided, as well as bookcases, which are behind glass and fitted with locks. The building-up of the library can be made the stimulus for much good work on the part of the students. They can sell the products of their handicraft in the workroom and purchase books with the proceeds, or use their studies in literature as basis for entertainments of various kinds. The older people of the district can also help collect books bearing on whatever subject will benefit the com-

munity at large in its various phases of activity.

The lighting of this building is from the back and left, so that the eyes of the pupils will not be put to needless strain, and the windows are casement, ample and attractive enough to satisfy the double purpose of use and ornament. There is desk room for fifty-six pupils, besides the kindergarten chairs at the low table, and the seating facilities can be greatly increased by extra chairs in the workroom when political and neighborhood meetings are held.

The study of botany should include practical demonstrations of flower-planting in the yard. A plot of ground can be set aside where wild flowers can be transplanted and cared for. Children can be taught to remove carefully a vigorous plant from among a colony of them where its loss will not be felt, and place it where its beauty will be fully enjoyed. They can study seed growth by growing garden flowers around their schoolhouse and thus learn also to beautify a place, a knowledge they will put to use in building their own homes later on.

The craftsmanship learned in the workroom can be put to various practical uses in the yard, so that all the pupils can have the pleasure of knowing they have helped to make the plot of ground set aside for them beautiful and serviceable. Classes in carpentry can be held in the yard, and fences built and gates made from designs of their own, perfected during the winter months in the school workroom, and demonstrations of practical forestry can be given when the flagpole is selected, felled, prepared and set up again.

In fact, a schoolhouse of this sort, while as simple and economic in design and construction as its rural location demands, should prove a very definite factor in the development of the community. We have merely suggested here a few of the ways in which the building and its facilities could be made of service to the pupils and their parents and friends, but other ways will no doubt suggest themselves with the increasing interest of the people in every department of their manual, mental and social life, and with their eagerness to keep in touch with the best of world progress.

CRAFTSMAN GARDENS FOR CRAFTSMAN HOMES

A CRAFTSMAN house should be surrounded by grounds that embody the Craftsman principles of utility, economy of effort and beauty. All these qualities it is possible for the average man to achieve in his garden by a little careful study and skilful planning. The majority of home owners today are people who must necessarily depend upon their own efforts for taking care of and beautifying their home grounds. As far as the men are concerned, they are as a rule workers in the city who could afford to give perhaps a part of Saturday and all day Sunday to any garden they had, with an occasional hour in the morning and the evening and holidays thrown in. This, of course, means that their gardens must be planned in such a way as to require the minimum amount of care and stand the maximum amount of neglect. In answer to the obvious question: "Since the time I could spend upon it is likely to be limited, could I really have much of a garden?" the answer is emphatically, "You can if you wish. You can have a most considerable garden of vegetables, flowers, fruit and berries that will quite fulfil the purposes of beauty and utility and give you a splendid outlet for your natural desire to grow things." The amount of ground you have is a ruling

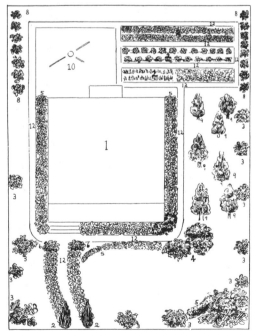

PLAN FOR PLANTING SPRING GARDEN: NO. 1.

factor, of course, in your plans, but even on the smallest suburban lot, say sixty by one hundred feet, perhaps less, a very satisfactory garden scheme can be worked out.

In order to illustrate practically just what can be done, we have taken four of our most popular designs for Craftsman houses and have made garden plans for them in which the most economical use of the surrounding land has been taken into consideration, and in which we have had regard also for beauty. In house number one we have taken a plot approximately seventy-five by one hundred feet and put on it a house that is about forty feet square, and we have pictured it as it would appear in the early spring. As will be noted, we have provided for a vegetable garden, a drying space, an orchard, a good-sized lawn and flower borders. In laying out the part devoted to vegetables we have suggested a large number of paths. These paths are almost a necessity. While they cut down the space, they make it possible for the home owner to hoe his vegetables without going up to his ankles in mud, and thus the garden is likely to get much more attention. The space as given does not seem large. It will, however, provide more vegetables than the average person would imagine, and would certainly grow sufficient of the staple vegetables to keep a family of four or five well supplied throughout the summer.

In choosing the vegetables you will plant, and, in fact, in considering the entire garden scheme, it is best to be careful not to plan for more than you can really take care of. Agree with yourself that you will be faithful to your garden; decide just how many hours you are sure you will be able to spend each week upon it, and err on the small side in making your estimate, rather than on the larger. Do not put into your vegetable garden things which will require a large amount of cultivating throughout the season, such as celery, which has to be banked up. Choose the standard things such as peas, beets, beans, green onions, carrots, spinach, radishes, limas, parsley, turnips, that practically can be had for the trouble of sowing, harvesting and a small amount of labor each week. Tomatoes, lettuce and asparagus require a little attention and should be added only after considerable thought. It is better not to have them than to have them come to nothing through neglect. You can have corn and squash and cabbage,

CRAFTSMAN HOUSE WITH SPRINGTIME GARDEN IN BLOOM: YELLOW PREDOMINATING: NO. 1.

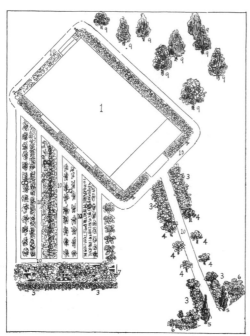

PLAN FOR PLANTING EARLY SUMMER GARDEN: NO. 2.

and perhaps muskmelons and watermelons, too, if your space permits. If you wish to add potatoes you must be able to provide considerable land and time for them.

It is well to bear in mind that horticulture specialists are all the time studying to produce varieties of vegetables, fruits and flowers that will stand bad conditions and neglect and be free from pests. It is wise to get the catalogues of good seedsmen, read them carefully for suggestions, because they are usually reliable, and select those varieties of flowers and vegetables which are quoted as most hardy.

Fruit and some small berries can be included in the garden of a Craftsman house. Recently very satisfactory dwarf fruit trees have been developed. You can get apples, peaches, cherries, plums and nectarines. They grow to about six feet and are very compact of form, and produce for their size a large amount of perfect, good-flavored fruit. They are especially suited to a Craftsman garden because, though like all fruit trees they must be sprayed and pruned, these processes involve the smallest amount of labor and can be done from the ground instead of from ladders. In plan number one we have placed these trees on the south side of the house where they will get the largest amount of sun. The best

small fruits for the Craftsman garden are gooseberries and currants. These bushes ask practically no attention. Raspberries are possible, but they require cutting down each year. Blackberries should be avoided because they have a tendency to run wild. The plan provides, as can be seen, a good piece of lawn close to the house. It is best that this should be kept practically open and free from small flower beds or shrubs, as these are troublesome when the lawn is being mowed.

The character and color of the house itself must be very carefully taken into consideration in choosing and planting the flowers, shrubs and trees. It goes without saying that a house should have some trees about it; if there are any already on the ground, so much the better; if not, of course, they must be furnished. Trees of a very satisfactory size, quite large enough to be really impressive, can be bought from any nursery, and if the home owner can afford nothing else he should at the outset afford several good trees. Evergreens, such as cedars, spruces, firs and arborvitæ are most satisfactory because they decorate the grounds the year through. On the plan we have indicated a cedar tree at each side of the front gate. These grow quite tall and have a pyramidal shape that suits them especially for flanking the gateway. Maples grow rather quickly and one placed close to the house might be added to this plan, to take away any sense of bareness from the façade. Birches, because of their beautiful white bark, are decorative even in winter, and one ought to be included among the trees planted. Dwarf Japanese cut-leaf maples have a beautiful red foliage in spring and fall, and a place should be found for at least one where it will be seen against evergreens, if possible.

The flower garden should be planned with a view to its harmonizing in color with the house. The first illustrated is brown with a dark red roof. Success in making the colors of the flowers harmonize with the house is merely a matter of careful thought and planning. One can have from flowers almost as many colors as a painter can mix on his palette, and one can have them from early spring until late fall, and in the winter one can have shrubs with beautiful red, yellow or green branches. What are known as hardy herbaceous plants are the most popular ones now, and justly so. They are the best ones for a Craftsman garden because they mean the smallest amount of

AN EARLY SUMMER CRAFTSMAN GARDEN IN ROSE, LAVENDER, BLUE AND WHITE: NO. 2.

171

trouble, and because they are likely to survive the largest amount of neglect. After they are once put out they stay in their places forever, and all they need is to be raked around with the hoe occasionally and to have their roots thinned out when they have begun to grow too thickly. Even when not in bloom they furnish decorative foliage to cover the bare earth. In planting the flowers make a careful selection so that you may have a succession of bloom and so that the colors of the flowers shall not clash with each other or clash with the house. Be careful not to put the magenta flowers against pink ones for example, or to have on the porch climbing roses that will not harmonize with the red of the roof, or purple against pink.

The suggestions we give for planting the garden of house number one will bring a general impression of a cheerful yellow all over the garden. In the garden scheme flowering shrubs must be included, and we have suggested here forsythia or golden bell as the most important shrub. To assist in giving the yellow effect we have included daffodils sprinkled thickly in the borders, also red and yellow tulips, yellow iris and yellow crocus. At each side of the steps we have placed a yellow peony. With these flowers in predom-

inance an especially bright and sunny effect will be produced in the springtime. In the beds there will, of course, be other hardy annuals showing their foliage to fill in the bare spots. These will come out later, but they naturally also should be planted with an understanding of the combination of color they will make at their period of bloom, and its relation to the house. The plot surrounding this house is seventy-five by one hundred feet, room enough for a small garden.

House number two is built of grayish brown stone and brown shingles, and has a dull-green roof. The plot on which it is located is of slightly irregular shape, as plots usually are in the better class of properties. It is about one hundred and fifty by two hundred feet and slopes slightly up from the northeast to a level space, on the edge of which the house is placed, facing southeast in order to get the sunlight in the living room, dining room and main bedrooms.

In making the plan for the flower planting we have had in mind the general appearance of the place in early summer. These are the months when one can expect to get the best out of one's roses. A delightful rose for a Craftsman garden is the Japanese variety usually called rugosa, which seems to be proof against all floral ailments. It produces flowers somewhat like the wild rose, only larger and richer in color, and has a thick, somewhat lustrous foliage that makes it very satisfactory as a shrub as well as a flower. It is being constantly developed, and the newer proved varieties are sure to be satisfactory to the Craftsman gardener. It produces large red seed-pods that are extremely decorative in the fall. Rugosa roses can be planted freely among the shrubs. A climbing rose is always a cheerful decoration to a house. It softens the lines and gives shade if allowed to run over the porch. Some varieties of climbing roses bloom with an almost miraculous profusion. As the roof of the house is a dark green, we would suggest in this case a deep pink climbing rose. Standard roses are those that have been grafted to the top of a sturdy trunk, and usually stand two or three feet high, bushing out at the top. These can be planted at the edges of a walk, as we suggest in this plan. They have a note of formality that is not too strong to harmonize with a Craftsman house.

The choice of shrubs offered for this time

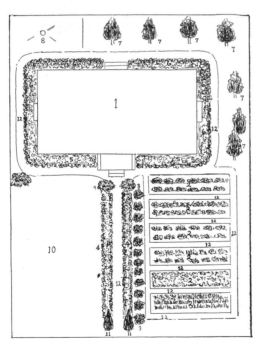

PLAN FOR PLANTING LATE SUMMER GARDEN: NO. 3.

A LATE SUMMER CRAFTSMAN GARDEN, WITH FLOWERS AND VEGETABLES SIDE BY SIDE   NO. 3.

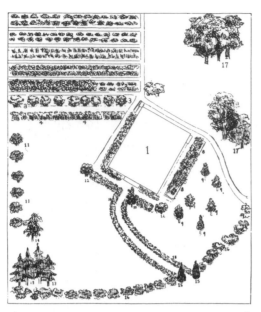

PLAN FOR PLANTING FALL GARDEN: NO. 4.

of the year is quite generous. We have in mind a scheme of coloring largely lavender and white. The key to this scheme will be set in shrubs by the lilacs which can be had in both white and lavender. There are Japanese snowballs, mock orange and spiræa for the note of white in the shrubs. Among the flowers, columbine, iris, forget-me-not and lily-of-the-valley will contribute to the general lavender and white effect, and will come in bloom in this period.

Grapes a Craftsman gardener can have without much trouble, and a grape arbor is included in the second plan. The vegetable garden is placed to the side and is screened from the road by the grape arbor, and gooseberry and currant bushes have been planted along another side to hide it partially from the main pathway to the house. If borders are placed on the lawn side of the arbor and the row of bushes the effect will be very satisfactory. There should also be borders in front of the house, and we have suggested that they run part of the way down the path from the house on both sides, and part of the way up from the gate on both sides, the standard roses serving to join the two effects of bloom. Poplar trees are of interesting shape, making slim pyramids, and are suitable to plant, as we have indicated in this plan, at the sides of the gateway. A low hedge of privet might be placed

at the edge of the lawn to separate it from the public roadway or sidewalk. Dwarf fruit trees would be effective on the slope at the east side of the house, and evergreens might be clustered behind the beds at the gateway and in the front corners of the plot. A maple tree and perhaps a birch might be planted close to the house.

An interesting arrangement of flowers for midsummer, that would harmonize with this house would be one emphasizing the blues and whites. This would make the garden seem cool during the hot July and August days when one prefers to have the red and yellow out of sight. The larkspurs, the campanulas or bell flowers, the aconitums or monkshoods, and the platycodons will make a good show of blue and white at this time. And among the shrubs deutzia and blue spiræa are in blossom.

Plan number three is made for the effect of late summer. One of the important features of this plan is the placing of the vegetable garden in front of the house. A properly kept vegetable garden is in its way as beautiful as a flower garden, and by treating it decoratively and letting it have here and there a few clumps of flowers, it can be made a very charming spot indeed. It will be in conformity with the Craftsman spirit that so essential a part of the home as the vegetable garden need not be hidden. In late summer this garden will have its vegetables well toward maturity, and if corn has been planted it will be showing its decorative foliage. As one method of marking the boundary of this vegetable garden we have placed gooseberry and currant bushes between it and the pathway to the house. The floral scheme consists of long borders at the edge of the path from the gate, and borders around the house. A few annuals, such as nasturtiums, poppies, asters and cosmos require so little attention that they can be used profusely in a Craftsman garden. This late summer plan calls for poppies at the front of the house. In the long borders beside the main walk the predominant flower is golden glow. Hollyhocks have been indicated in the beds at the side of the house. Unless somewhat protected from heavy winds, these are likely to be damaged, and so a sheltered location such as the one indicated is best. The plot for this garden is seventy-five by one hundred feet.

The substantial house we have chosen in

174

A BRILLIANT FALL CRAFTSMAN GARDEN, FOR LITTLE LABOR AND MONEY: TONE RED AND PURPLE: NO. 4.

this case is of cement with brownish yellow stone and a brown roof. The general effect of the flowers in the garden will harmonize well with this house, since the predominant colors are a warm yellow and white. Rose of Sharon is a good-sized shrub that blossoms in late summer. The white variety would be best for this planting. The house faces the north, and the dwarf fruit trees are placed to the south and west. The evergreens and other trees could be planted at the edges of the plot with the shrubs in between. An interesting arrangement would be to have little round box bushes flanking the gateway, and Rose of Sharon on each side of the pathway in front of the house.

The fourth garden plan contains suggestions for planting with fall effects in mind. Here again the house is on an irregularly shaped piece of property and on the brow of a slight slope. This piece of ground is about two hundred and twenty-five feet by one hundred and seventy-five feet, and the house is placed to face the northwest. The garden occupies ground to the northeast and is partly screened by gooseberry and currant bushes, before which is a flower border. In the front of the house are two borders with a path between, the one closest the house being filled with nasturtiums that keep up their bloom until frost, and the other devoted largely to red, white and yellow chrysanthemums. The path down to the gate is also fringed with nasturtiums.

One of the most beautiful fall flowers—an annual, by the way—is salvia. It is so wonderful in color that one can hardly afford to do without it, but it must be started indoors in March in "flats." Its color is so decided that it kills nearly everything else, and so should be very carefully handled. We have indicated salvia on one side of the house, where it will be seen almost alone and not clash with other flowers. Cosmos will last till frost and might be planted in the border shielding the vegetable garden, in some strong deep reds that would stand the proximity of the brilliant salvia. The grape arbor is placed to the southwest of the house, and the orchard of dwarf fruit trees on the slope to the southwest. What is known as Japanese barberry, that turns an exquisite deep red in the fall, makes a hedge of moderate height. This might be used to divide the lawn from the roadway. About the only shrub that can be

counted on at this time of the year is the hardy hydrangea, and we have suggested one placed at each end of the second border before the house. The Japanese cut-leaf maples have a gorgeous foliage in fall, and a good specimen tree of this would be effective near the house.

This is the time of the year when evergreens will be most useful, and a house to be occupied in the fall should have clumps of such trees planted about.

SCHEDULES OF PLANTING FOR EARLY SPRING GARDEN. 1.—House. 2.—Cedars. 3.—Shrubs: forsythia, spiræa, deutzia, etc. 4.—Banks of rose-bushes: Red, yellow and white rugosas. 5.—Border beds of hardy flowers: Daffodils, iris, crocus, tulips in bloom, backed by other flowers such as larkspur, columbine, phlox, bell flower. 6.—Peony bushes. 7.—Plots with vegetables. 8.—Gooseberry and currant bushes. 9.—Dwarf fruit trees in bloom. 10.—Drying ground. 11.—Lawn. 12.—Walks. (See page 168.)

SCHEDULE OF PLANTING FOR EARLY SUMMER GARDEN. 1.—House. 2.—Border: Lily-of-the-valley close to house, phlox. 3.—Border: Sweet-william, iris, phlox, etc. 4.—Standard rose-bushes. 5.—Poplars. 6.—Shrubs: Japanese snow-ball, mock-orange, spiræa, backed by small evergreens. 7.—Grape arbor. 8.—Vegetable garden. 9.—Dwarf fruit trees. 10.—Walks. 11.—Currant and gooseberry bushes. (See page 170.)

SCHEDULE OF PLANTING FOR LATE SUMMER GARDEN. 1.—House. 2.—Vegetable garden. 3.—Currant and gooseberry bushes. 4.—Borders with phlox and golden glow as main flower. 5.—Border with poppies. 6.—Borders with hollyhocks. 6a.—Lilies in the vegetable garden. 7.—Dwarf fruit trees. 8.—Drying yard. 9.—Rose of Sharon. 10.—Lawn. 11.—Pyramidal box bushes at gateway. 12.—Walks. (See page 172.)

SCHEDULE OF PLANTING FOR FALL GARDEN. 1.—House. 2.—Vegetable plot,—corn prominent. 3.—Currant and gooseberry bushes. 4.—Border with red and white cosmos. 5.—Border of salvia. 6.—Border of nasturtiums. 7.—Border with chrysanthemums: Red, white and yellow. 8. — Grape arbor. 9. — Dwarf fruit trees. 10. — Japanese cut-leaf maple. 11. — Shrubs. 12. — Hardy hydrangeas. 13.—Evergreens. 14.—Birch or pin oak. 15.—Pyramidal privets. 16.—Japanese barberry hedge. 17.—Old trees. (See page 174.)

PERGOLAS IN AMERICAN GARDENS

A DOUBLE PERGOLA, VINE-COVERED AND ROSE-GROWN: THE OVERHEAD POLES OF THE PERGOLA ARE OF CEDAR, AND THEIR RUSTIC EFFECT IS IN KEEPING WITH THE PLANTING SCHEME AND IN PLEASING CONTRAST TO THE FORMAL LINES OF THE HALF-TIMBER OF THE HOUSE FROM WHOSE PORCH THE PERGOLA STRETCHES FORTH.

WHATEVER connects a house with out of doors, whether vines or flowers, piazza or pergola, it is to be welcomed in the scheme of modern home-making. We need outdoor life in this country; we need it inherently, because it is the normal thing for all people, and we need it specifically as a nation, because we are an overwrought people, too eager about everything except peace and contentment. I wonder if anyone reading this article has ever in life received the following invitation, "Will you come and sit in my garden with me this afternoon?" I doubt it very much, at least in America. In England this would happen, or in Italy, and I think in Bavaria the people rest in their gardens at the close of the day and grow strong and peaceful with the odor of flowers about them, and the songs of birds. In a garden the silence teaches the restless spirit peace, and Nature broods over man and heals the wounds of the busy world. In essence a garden is a companion, a physician, a philosopher. It is equally the place for the happy, the sorrowing, for the successful, for the despondent.

And so here in America of all things we need gardens, and we must so plan our gardens that we shall live in them, and we must have in them our favorite flowers, long pathways of them, which lead us from gate to doorstep, and we must enter our gateway under fragrant bowers. We must build up arbors for our fruit, rustic shelter for our children, and above all these things our garden, which should be our outdoor home, must surely have a pergola, a living place outdoors that is beautiful in construction, that is draped in vines, that gives us green walls to live within, that has a ceiling of tangled leaves and flowers blowing in the wind, a glimpse of blue sky through open spaces and sunshine pouring over us when the leaves move.

PERGOLAS IN AMERICAN GARDENS

With a pergola in the garden you can no more escape living out of doors than you can avoid swimming in the sea if you happily chance to be living on the edge of the ocean. A pergola focuses your garden life. It is like a fireplace in a living room; it is the spirit of the outdoor environment held in one place to welcome you. It is essentially a place in which to rest, or to play or to do quiet domestic tasks; it is the outdoor home for children, for old folks, a spot in which to dream waking dreams or to sleep happily, or, best of all, for on the other hand, as in one of the illustrations, it gracefully hides a group of unbeautiful farm buildings. It may lead to a beautiful garden or out to a wonderful view, or it may be the culmination of the garden scheme and furnish the only vista of which limited grounds are capable. It epitomizes modern outdoor life, and its beauty is through simplicity of construction and intimacy with Nature. A pergola inevitably means good simple lines of construction, beautified with vines, hidden with fruit or flowers, and with sunlight in splashes

SHOWING THE USE OF PERGOLAS TO HIDE IN A PICTURESQUE FASHION THE OUTBUILDINGS OF A FARM: THIS PICTURE IS A REPRODUCTION OF THE PERGOLAS AT THE STETSON FARMS, STERLINGTON, N. Y.

romance. For a pergola is a wonderfully inspiring spot in twilight, or when moonlit.

The outdoor living place is suited equally to any landscape or climate. It can be adjusted to any kind of architecture. It can be built directly with the house, a part of the architectural scheme, as in the original Italian pergolas, or it may be half-hidden at the end of a garden or creeping along the edge of the woods. It may convert a path into a cloister or a grape arbor into a summer house. It has many traditions but no formal rules.

It has been used as a triumphant architectural feature in a modern country house; on the foliage, pillars, furniture and floor.

As we have already said, in construction a pergola may relate closely to the architecture of the house, or on the other hand it may suggest an ornamental addition of a later date and be developed in materials different from the house, or it may bear no relation whatever to the house construction. The adobe pergola is a fascinating feature of many of the Pacific Slope houses; yet one often sees the adobe house with a pergola or pergola porch of redwood, designed on straight lines with Japanese effect. In New England and on Long Island the pergola with brick sup-

178

PERGOLAS IN AMERICAN GARDENS

PERGOLA-PORCH FOR A COUNTRY HOUSE AT EAST HAMPTON, LONG ISLAND: THE PERGOLA PORCH IS RAPIDLY TAKING THE PLACE OF THE OLD-TIME PIAZZA.

PERGOLAS IN AMERICAN GARDENS

ports and wooden overhead beams is most usual, while out in New Jersey more often you find the pergola used in place of a porch, possibly a new feature of a quaint old house, and built of ordinary lumber, just as one would construct a trellis or a fruit arbor.

As a matter of fact, a pergola attached to the house is an ideal substitute for a piazza. This is especially true where there is the slightest tendency for the rooms to be somewhat dark, as it affords a decorative finish to the house, a charming resting place, a picturesque opportunity for vines, and yet permits all possible sunlight to reach the windows.

In one of the illustrations in this article the cement supports of the pergola are topped with rustic poles heavily draped with vines, and the effect is most picturesque. In fact, an entire rustic pergola is charming in an informal simple garden. It has, however, the drawback of not being as free from insects and dampness as the concrete structures.

As for the pergola "drapery," there is seemingly no limit to the beautiful things which the concrete or stone or brick columns will support. In the Far West some of the most beautiful pergolas are almost bowers of tea roses, intertwined with wistaria and monthly honeysuckle. In the East it is necessary to use the hardier roses, the Ramblers in different hues, white and red and pink. Wistaria is also one of the most attractive pergola vines when combined with others of the more hardy foliage and later bloom. It is difficult to get the monthly blooming honeysuckle in the East, but it proves most graceful as a pergola covering where it can be secured. Through the North, such vines as ivy, clematis and woodbine are all satisfactory, and nothing is more delightful than a pergola covered with grapevines, where the location and latitude are suitable, for the bloom of the grape is ineffable in the spring, the foliage is heavy through the summer and the fragrance and color of the fruit delicious in the fall. The delicately leaved jessamine with its sweet blossoms, the Allegheny vine, even more lace-like in foliage and graced by bells of white, the canary vine of yellow-orchid beauty, are unequaled for small, slender pergolas. The wild cucumber should be better known and appreciated, and also the bittersweet with its clusters of sweet white blossoms of springlike beauty, and its orange berries that break asunder at the first frost and reveal scarlet fruit which hang together, orange and scarlet, even when snow outlines twig and branch. The hop with its pale green pendant seed pods should be more in evidence in our garden as a decorative vine. The ornamental gourd is a quick-growing vine that can flourish verdantly while other vines are starting their slower climb, and its strange fruit can be put to a number of charming uses. The Dutchman's pipe is a vine whose curious flowers will repay cultivation.

It is always wise, in planning your garden, to plant about a pergola from two to four kinds of flower-bearing or fruit-bearing vines, so that each season will have its fragrance and color. It is also interesting to plant rows of shrubs at the foot of the supports and between the supports, that the whole structure may be more intimately connected with the ground.

Some pergolas are completely hidden by vines festooned from pillar to pillar; this is especially satisfactory in very hot climates. While others have vines twining only about the pillars with adequate protection overhead. This is by far the more classical and intrinsically beautiful method of treating a pergola. It has the disadvantage, however, of leaving the inner portion of the pergola a little less restful and homelike than when curtained by vines and shrubs.

For the newly built pergola there are many quick-growing vines which will give it a green and cheerful effect the first season,—morning-glo-

PERGOLA OF COBBLESTONES AND RUSTIC, WITH WISTARIA VINES.

PERGOLAS IN AMERICAN GARDENS

A PERGOLA-ARBOR, SHOWING AN INTERESTING APPLICATION OF THE PERGOLA IDEA TO AN OLD-FASHIONED GRAPE ARBOR, ESPECIALLY ADAPTED TO THE MORE SIMPLE TYPE OF COUNTRY ARCHITECTURE.

ries, scarlet runners, clematis, with castor beans at the entrance and geraniums at the sides and you have by July the effect of many years' growth.

Pergola gateways are attractive when bowered by flowering vines, and a driveway arched at the entrance with a simple pergola has charm hard to excel. A division or retaining wall can be redeemed from monotony by using it as one side of a pergola, constructing the pillars of brick if the wall is of brick, or of stone or concrete if the wall is of either of these materials. The rafters can be of rustic or square-hewn beams. Such treatment of a wall would have quite the spirit of cloister walks, and seats built in would heighten this monastic quality.

As to the materials to be used in construction of all pergolas, the resources of the immediate locality should be drawn upon in preference to all others. Stone piers built of cobble will be most suitable to one neighborhood, while split stone is better in another, and in some places it would be possible to have them

of whole field stone. Pillars of rough brick are decoratively valuable at times, terra cotta at others, cement at still others. They can be placed singly, in pairs or in groups to harmonize with the surrounding type of garden and house.

Turned wooden columns of classic design, either plain or fluted, are favorite supports for trellised roofs. Rustic pillars of cedar, fir, white pine, cypress, oak, madrone, redwood, with girders of the same wood a trifle small in size, are unequalled for informal gardens. Rustic is the most inexpensive material of which a pergola can be built, if it can be obtained with little cost of transportation, the square wooden supports coming next in order. Satisfactory combinations are sometimes devised, such as cement pillars and eucalyptus rafters and girders, stone supports with wooden rafters and trellis of various woods.

To preserve the true pergola form, to keep it from becoming an arbor, the trellis strips must not be put on horizontally between the pillars—this is the chief distinguishing note

PERGOLAS IN AMERICAN GARDENS

and must not be transgressed. Vines may be draped from pillar to pillar and not mar the purity of type, or trellis strips may be placed against the pillars, parallel with them, for vines to clamber upon, and purity of style be intact, but the horizontal feature must not appear upon the pergola—unless you want an arbor.

It is an excellent idea to plan a pergola with built-in seats at the sides and with rustic permanent tables, also with rough flooring for damp days. The joy of this garden feature is its livableness, to get the full satisfaction of which it must be a convenient homelike place for reading, sewing, afternoon tea, children's games. And of all things it should be the ideal spot for the writer or for the student, for working out of doors means working with health, and as a health-giving feature the properly constructed, properly draped pergola is second only to that other most wholesome development of modern building, the outdoor sleeping porch.

The pole pergola is a sort of pergola that is especially adapted to rustic surroundings, and many a restored cottage on abandoned farms has been made lovely by the introduction of such a feature, the poles having been cut from woodlot saplings. Even where all the materials had to be purchased,—cedar posts, plants, and the labor counted in—twelve or fifteen dollars, depending upon locality, would be fully sufficient to cover the whole cost.

The pergola-arbor illustrated on page one hundred and eighty-one is from the cottage of Mr. Frederick C. Keppel at Montrose, New York, designed by Edward Shepard Hewitt. For a pergola-arbor of this sort there could be no lovelier covering than the wild-grape, or the wild clematis, and, again, the kudzu vine, which comes to us from Japan and is found to be perfectly hardy everywhere, will, by reason of its extraordinarily rapid growth and luxuriant foliage of enormous rich green leaves, prove especially useful where a quick effect is desired.

The illustration on page one hundred and seventy-nine of a pergola porch on a country house at East Hampton, Long Island, exhibits another form of the pergola which requires far more restraint in planting, for it is intended that it should stand forth itself as an architectural feature; hence the vine-growth here will never be permitted completely to obscure the design of its support. The two great jars of terra-cotta add striking notes to the pergola and make this, in design, a successful house approach.

The pergola illustrated on page one hundred and seventy-eight is one connected with the outbuildings on the Stetson Farms, Sterlington, New York, designed by Alfred Hopkins. Here has been presented the problem of making the pergola serve, not only as a screen, but as a support for an overhead cartage rail which serves to facilitate the removal of stable litter expeditiously, neatly and hidden from observation. Ultimately the planting here will form a complete screen, summer and winter.

A PLEASANT VISTA OF APPROACH FORMED BY PERGOLA WITH RUSTIC ROOF SUPPORTED BY PILLARS OF CEMENT.

TWO BRICK BUNGALOWS WITH CYPRESS GABLES

Published in The Craftsman, February, 1912.

ROOMY ONE-STORY BRICK BUNGALOW: NO. 129.

BRICK is undoubtedly advancing in favor as a building material for houses. This is not only because people are demanding a more permanent form of home architecture, but because the wood supply of the country is becoming a matter for serious consideration, and some material must be found to take the place of wood, which is equally or even more satisfactory.

Brick nowadays is much more beautiful and durable than formerly. It shows significant signs of eventually superseding wood, at least in the exterior construction of houses, and is becoming a feature of interior finish as well. It is adapted to almost any style of building, whether large or small, furnishing a delightful note of color to any landscape, and carrying a distinct and pleasing individuality. Although the first expense of building a brick house is somewhat greater than that of a frame house, yet in the end it is decidedly the more economical, for after it is once finished it requires almost no additional expense to keep it in order, while a frame house requires constant repairing and painting. Is it not much more profitable to build better and repair less? Besides, there are other advantages. A brick house is more easily heated during the winter, and is far cooler in summer than a frame house.

Brick being practically fireproof, the rate of insurance is less, and being more durable the building does not deteriorate in value so quickly.

Perhaps one of the most notable things about modern brick is the way it is laid up, for the result is so much more interesting and beautiful than with the old-time method. The old brick was of a uniform red, laid up with a narrow white joint. This mortar was made of fine sand, cement and lime, and the joints were very narrow and pointed smooth. Sometimes these joints were painted a glaring white so there was no mistaking the regularity and perfection of the bond. But the modern brick is far removed from this, for the aim now is to avoid startling contrasts and pronounced colors. If the house is to be of red brick, they are used in many different harmonious tones; if of buff brick, they are in shades of old buff, golden brown and deep cream. These are placed in position about as they come, care being taken not to put together any two of a like tone. This gives an indescribable variety to the wall, an effect of great uniformity of tone, yet full of interest that is far superior to the monotonous solid red wall of old time.

The new mortar is made to produce a texture similar to that of the brick and is often

TWO BRICK BUNGALOWS WITH CYPRESS GABLES

one-third or one-half the thickness of the brick. This innovation is made practical by the improved method of the mixture. "Grit," sand, cement, lime and coloring matter are mixed according to an exact formula. The "grit" consists of small pebbles screened from sand in order to allow a perfect measuring of sand and "grit." The sand is coarse and sharp and is never taken from a beach, for in the spring the effervescing of salt water causes an unpleasant disfigurement of the wall.

We give one formula for mixing mortar, and it is hardly necessary to add that any for-

trowel, and the "raked out joint" made by cutting the joint back from the surface of the brick with the point of the trowel, a nail or a bit of wood. In both cases the mortar should show as much texture as the brick.

Believing, therefore, that there are great possibilities for durability and beauty in the modern use of brick, we have planned here two bungalows which embody several new ideas in brick construction. The use of brick in the interior as well as the exterior of these bungalows is of especial interest, and we are giving several drawings which show in detail

GLIMPSE OF LIVING ROOM, INGLENOOK AND DINING ROOM IN BUNGALOW NO. 129, SHOWING UNIQUE METHOD OF INTERIOR CONSTRUCTION INCLUDING THE USE OF BRICK, PLASTER AND WOOD FOR PARTITIONS AND WALLS.

mula used must be strictly adhered to throughout the building, so that no variation of shade mars the perfection:

"Grit" 3	parts
Sand 5	"
Cement 1	"
Lime Putty (hydrated lime)........ ½	"
Brown (paste) .... ⅓	"
Yellow (powder) .... ⅓	"
Black (paste) 1/50	"

The joints are finished in many ways, though the most frequently used are the "rough cut flush," made by allowing the mortar to ooze out beyond the surface of the brick and then cutting it off with a sharp, quick stroke of the

the great decorative effect obtained by this new method. Rough-surfaced, hard-baked brick, of several harmonious tones of red or brown, is to be used, which gives a rich sense of warm friendly color decidedly different from the old-time lifeless red.

In the exterior of these bungalows the brick has been combined with stone, relieved by wood in the upper story and by the ornamental as well as structural use of heavy beams. A detailed floor plan of the porch of the first house, No. 129, is given, showing how an interesting combination of concrete, brick and stone can be made. Dividing the floor space into three sections by the use of brick brings about a charming decorative effect, while the

TWO BRICK BUNGALOWS WITH CYPRESS GABLES

low stone balustrade gives a sense of seclusion and permits a note of color to appear in the form of flowers or ferns placed upon the low corner posts.

Formerly the brick walls of a house were laid up in an eight- or twelve-inch solid wall, and the plaster was put directly on the inside of the wall. A wall constructed in this way sweats, so it was found necessary to furr it, leaving an air space between the brick wall and the plaster.

The walls of these bungalows are made by erecting two four-inch walls, side by side, leaving a two-inch space between. These walls are tied together by metal tie straps inserted every few courses. This provides a good air space all around the house, giving perfect insulation from heat and cold, and at the same time it allows the use of fancy brick for the inside wall, which considerably lessens the expense of building. The cost of furring will be saved also, for the plaster can be put directly on the inside wall, as the air space will prevent condensation of moisture, or sweating. The partitions of these houses are of brick, the wall at the baseboard, side and head casings being eight inches thick, while the panels between are only four inches thick. These panels are plastered on both sides, leaving a reveal between the plastered panels and casings of

about one and one-quarter inches. Doors and windows are hung on jambs only, expensive frames and trim being thus saved. This treatment of the walls gives æsthetic quality to the whole interior.

The use of brick in the interior of a house not only lends it decorative charm and individuality, but is a source of economy. The in-

FLOOR PLAN OF ONE-STORY BRICK BUNGALOW: NO. 129.

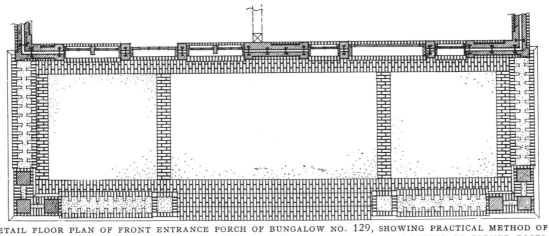

DETAIL FLOOR PLAN OF FRONT ENTRANCE PORCH OF BUNGALOW NO. 129, SHOWING PRACTICAL METHOD OF CONSTRUCTION, DECORATIVE USE OF BRICK AND CONCRETE, AND EFFECTIVE GROUPING OF CORNER POSTS.

TWO BRICK BUNGALOWS WITH CYPRESS GABLES

Published in The Craftsman, February, 1912.   BRICK BUNGALOW WITH PORCHES AND PERGOLA COURT: NO. 130.

terior wood finish of a house is always expensive, because it requires skilled labor, the best of materials, and cannot be done quickly.

The main walls only of these houses have been planned to be built of brick, but where partitions are only suggested—as between the living and dining rooms and inglenook of the first bungalow, No. 129—we have used the post and panel construction in wood. As the interior view shows, wooden ceiling beams mark the division between the rooms and run around the walls above the brick frieze; and the built-in seats and bookshelves of the nook, as well as the long window seat in the dining room, are all of wood, the seats being paneled with V-jointed boards. Not only does this use of woodwork add to the friendly quality of the interior, but it serves as a link between the structural features, built-in fittings and the rest of the furniture, while the combined effect of the brick, plaster and wood gives to the rooms an interesting sense of variety of textures and materials, and yet does not mar the underlying harmony of the whole.

The unity introduced into a room by a consistent color scheme is not, however, the only necessary element of harmony. Another factor is needed: namely, design. Now brick not only furnishes the uniformity of color requisite to carry out whatever tone harmony is desired, but it can also be laid in a pattern which will either emphasize the prevailing style of the room or else be in itself the suggestive or dominating note. Brick as now manufactured lends itself to various forms of design, for it comes in so many sizes that almost any geometric pattern can be carried out with it, and the finished frieze, support or arch will have almost the quality of a mosaic.

A frieze such as we have designed in these two bungalows, running around the whole room, has therefore the double interest of pleasing color and design. The interior view of bungalow No. 129 and the details given of the two fireplaces in the second bungalow, No. 130, illustrate the decorative results of this method of wall treatment. If the bricks are well chosen as to color and laid with good judgment and taste, they are most effective, and add to a room a rich note not unlike that of old tapestries. They can be laid in many patterns, intricate or simple, according to the

186

TWO BRICK BUNGALOWS WITH CYPRESS GABLES

PERGOLA COURT WITH CENTRAL FOUNTAIN IN BUNGALOW NO. 130: A MOST INVITING SPOT FOR OUTDOOR LIFE.

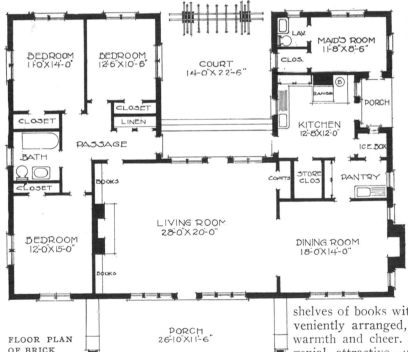

FLOOR PLAN OF BRICK BUNGALOW NO. 130.

desire of the owner. We are showing three simple styles that are both practical and pleasing.

In planning the floor space of the first bungalow, No. 129, convenience—always an important item in home building—was carefully considered, and a study of the plan will reveal how satisfactorily it has all been worked out. A roomy, pleasant, homelike atmosphere is noticed on entering the house, brought about partly by the view from the large living room into the bright sunny dining room, and the cozy nook by the fireplace with shelves of books within easy reach, lights conveniently arranged, and an open fire to give warmth and cheer. The whole effect is rich, genial, attractive—qualities so endearing in a home that they become another cause of desire for permanence.

187

TWO BRICK BUNGALOWS WITH CYPRESS GABLES

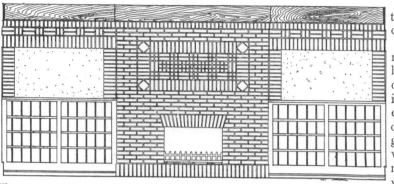

WALL IN LIVING ROOM OF BUNGALOW NO. 130, SHOWING USE OF BRICK IN CHIMNEYPIECE AND AROUND THE ROUGH PLASTER PANELS OVER THE BOOKCASES.

Every convenience has been planned for the kitchen. The pantry, which is indispensable for serving and prevents the kitchen odors from entering the dining room, is fitted with a sink and a drain board on each side. Another sink and large drainboard are placed in the kitchen under the windows so that plenty of light can be had at this necessary working place. The range is within easy reach, a good-sized store-room is provided, and even a cheerful kitchen porch, which serves the combined purpose of separating the maid's sleeping room from the kitchen, giving access to the refrigerator, and holding extra vegetables and different working accessories of the kitchen.

The bedrooms are shut off from the kitchen side of the house and the bath is placed conveniently. Not a particle of space is wasted in this plan, which includes living room, dining room, kitchen, maid's room, three other bedrooms, hall, bathroom, many closets and two porches, either of which is large enough for an outside living room in summer.

The floor plan of the second bungalow, No. 130, is if anything even more interesting than the first one. This gives a large living room with a dining room which is practically an extension of it. As one enters this room a direct view is had into the open pergola court, and also the fireplaces of both rooms can be seen, which gives a combined sense of home comfort and outdoor delight. The color of this room, brought about by the rich tones of the rough-surfaced brick, is especially restful, and the light from the fireplaces and from the windows that open onto the court add to the warmth and cheerfulness of its welcome.

The placing of the bedrooms upon one side of the house and the kitchen and dining room upon the other is particularly happy, for each is thus practically shut off from the other. The pergola court with hanging vines and splashing fountain makes a delightful passageway between the two divisions. A small hall near the living room permits indirect entrance into the bedrooms, thus giving a desired sense of privacy. The kitchen is provided with a convenient and pleasant little porch, similar to the one in No. 129. And there is also a large ice-box, pantry, store closets, two sinks, with the maid's room within

DINING-ROOM WALL IN BUNGALOW NO. 130, WITH PRACTICAL AND DECORATIVE BRICK CONSTRUCTION IN CHIMNEY, WALLS AND FRIEZE.

easy reach, yet separated by the porch. There is a similar number of rooms in each house, the court of one taking the place of the second porch of the other, but the arrangement of the given space is decidedly different in each bungalow; each one is attractive in an individual way to suit the needs or pleasures of different people, yet both are practical and homelike.

These bungalows have been designed especially for Eastern climates and are therefore fitted with Craftsman fireplace-furnaces which thoroughly heat and ventilate each building.

CONCRETE BUNGALOWS: ECONOMY OF CONSTRUCTION ATTAINED BY THE WAY THE FORMS ARE USED

I AM presenting here two Craftsman bungalows embodying a practical and economical idea in concrete construction. I believe that this new method, which is illustrated with perspective views and working drawings, will mean a reduction in cost and an increase in efficiency over the methods hitherto used, and so will be of interest to architects, builders and all who are considering the problem of building a home.

In order to make clear this new process of construction it may be well to explain briefly those usually employed. When concrete was first used it was found to be an ideal building material, indestructible and fireproof. The problem, however, was just *how* to use it to the best advantage. Solid concrete walls were built at first, but these had a serious disadvantage. Concrete is a good conductor of heat and cold and is affected by changes of temperature and varying atmospheric conditions. In winter, therefore, the cold air outside the house chilled the solid concrete walls, making the inner surface colder than the air within the rooms; whereupon the warm air within the house, coming in contact with the cool wall, was at once chilled, decreasing its moisture-holding capacity and causing the surplus moisture to condense upon the cool inner surface and run down the walls. This is what is known as sweating, and the dampness produced not only made the rooms chilly and unwholesome, but also stained and discolored the wall coverings and hangings.

Various methods were devised in an attempt to obviate this difficulty and to construct a solid concrete wall which would not sweat. Furring was used—that is to say, strips of wood were placed at intervals against the inner surface of the solid concrete wall, and lath and plaster were applied, the air space left between the concrete and the plaster serving as an insulation and thus preventing sweating. This construction, however, besides not being fireproof, involved the extra cost of wood and plaster, much time and labor, and so has never been considered quite satisfactory. Such a structure, moreover, is not ideal from an architectural standpoint, for it represents an attempt to remedy or cover up the defects of an unsatisfactory structure by imposing a superstructure not so durable.

At the present time one of the most widely used and efficient forms of concrete construction is the hollow concrete block. But even in this a serious objection is present, for although the hollow spaces extend vertically through the blocks at close intervals, and thus provide frequent air spaces between the inner and outer surfaces of the completed wall, the sides of the blocks which form the divisions between the holes still serve as a connection between the inner and outer surfaces of the wall, forming an occasional but nevertheless active conductor of heat and cold. The wall is thus only partially insulated, and sweating takes place to some extent wherever this solid connection occurs.

Concrete walls have also been made so as to include a continuous insulating air space, but these have either been cast in one piece or else expensive interchangeable metal forms have been used, and both methods, though efficient, have rendered the cost of construction high.

The only drawback to this last method being its expense, I have worked upon the theory that the most satisfactory form of concrete wall is one which can be cast with a continuous vertical air space, or other insulation, between two thicknesses of concrete, yet built

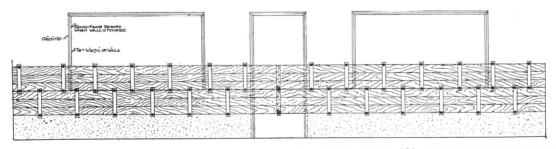

FIG. 1: ELEVATION OF FRONT OUTER WALL OF LIVING ROOM IN BUNGALOW NO. 131, IN PROCESS OF CONSTRUCTION, SHOWING DOOR AND WINDOW FRAMES SET IN WOODEN FORMS PREPARATORY TO FILLING IN CONCRETE.

189

Published in The Craftsman, March, 1912.

ONE-STORY CONCRETE BUNGALOW WITH SHINGLED GABLE AND RUBEROID ROOF: THE CONSTRUCTION IS ESPECIALLY ECONOMICAL OWING TO THE WAY IN WHICH THE WOODEN FORMS ARE USED IN CASTING THE CONCRETE WALLS (SEE WORKING DRAWINGS): NO. 131.

ECONOMICAL CONCRETE CONSTRUCTION

in such a way as to necessitate only the simplest, fewest and least expensive forms possible. I have decided, therefore, to use wooden forms, which cost much less than the metal ones and can be put up right on the building site by any carpenter, the forms being interchangeable, so that they may be used again and again as the wall is gradually built up, thus minimizing the number of forms required. I have also tried to devise reinforcing ties that would be sufficiently strong and yet as simple and economical as possible.

In designing the two bungalows which illustrate this new process, I have omitted the cellars because this permits a concrete foundation on which the concrete partitions of the house can be built. The omission of a cellar is a considerable saving of time, labor and materials, and if the bungalows are heated and ventilated by a Craftsman fireplace-furnace the only excavation needed would be for the ashpit. If a different heating system is desired, however, with the furnace located in the cellar, a sufficient space can be excavated for this purpose, in which case, of course, the coal bin would be included in the cellar instead of being on the ground floor. But if the cellar is used the usual wooden partitions would be built instead of the solid concrete partitions shown in these bungalows, as the excavation would prevent the use of the concrete foundation needed as a base for the concrete walls.

With the form of concrete construction used here, a trench is dug for the base of the outside walls. This trench is made deep enough to carry the walls below frost level, and the foundation walls are built up to the height desired. The ground enclosed by these walls is leveled off, covered with a layer of cinders, and on top of this is poured a layer of concrete. Nailing strips, 2 x 2, to which the wood flooring of the house may be nailed, are placed in this concrete layer while it is still soft, and the concrete which fills the spaces between these strips is leveled off flush with the top of them. This hardens and forms an inexpensive, practical and sanitary foundation. The exterior concrete walls extending below frost level prevent any frost from penetrating beneath the floors of the bungalow; the bed of cinders forms an insulation by taking up any

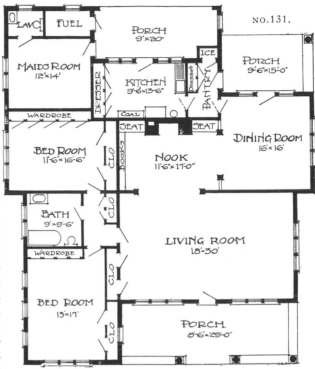

FLOOR PLAN OF CRAFTSMAN CONCRETE BUNGALOW.

moisture, and the concrete layer beneath the flooring gives the necessary base for the concrete partition walls of the interior.

The walls—which are preferably of cinder concrete—are cast in wooden forms. Each form consists of matched sheathing boards ⅞ inch thick and 5½ inches wide—known as the ordinary 6-inch sheathing boards—three of which are fitted together as shown to make each side of the form, which is thus 16½ inches deep. These three boards are then fastened together by wooden strips or cleats, D, nailed to the form at intervals of about 24 inches as shown in Figure 3, which represents part of two of the forms during the casting operation. Bolts are provided which extend through the cleats and sides of the form, each bolt head having two projections or pins, and a beveled washer, B, being inserted between the head of the bolt and the inner side of the form, as shown in Figure 2. The outer end of the bolt has the usual washer and nut which may be screwed up to secure the parts rigidly in place.

Three similarly joined boards are held in place opposite the first, to make the other side

191

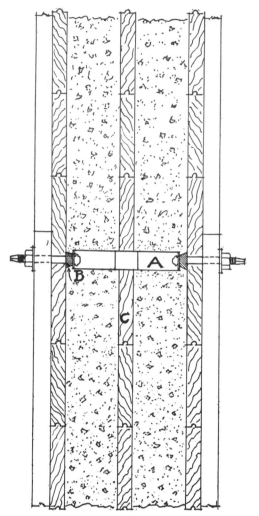

FIG. 2: VERTICAL SECTION THROUGH TWO OF THE WOODEN FORMS USED IN CONSTRUCTION OF BUNGALOWS NOS. 131 AND 132, SHOWING CENTRAL INSULATING BOARDS EMBEDDED IN CONCRETE AND HELD IN PLACE BY METAL REINFORCING TIE.

of the form, the two sides being 8 inches apart, with the central insulating boards, C, between and parallel with them. These are also sheathing boards, the same as those used for the sides of the form. These boards are selected because they are comparatively inexpensive and are always carried in stock, and by having the outside forms and the central insulating boards of corresponding sizes, the work of building up and casting the walls is greatly simplified. Before using these insulating boards they should be soaked in water for 24 hours, which will bring them to their maximum swelling point. Thus, when they are embedded in the concrete wall, they will shrink and become somewhat loose, leaving a slight air space on either side and so more completely insulating the concrete surfaces. Three of these boards are fitted together and temporarily fastened by means of wooden laths, and a saw notch is made in the edge of each outside board to receive the metal tie which is to hold the parts together. This reinforcing tie, A, which is $1\frac{1}{2}$ inches wide and $\frac{1}{8}$ inch thick. is bent in the center, as seen in the drawings, in order to hold the insulating boards in position and prevent any side motion of them during the casting operation. The ends of this tie are bent and provided with holes having opposite notches which register with projections or pins on the heads of the bolts. This allows the bolt heads of each wooden form to be passed through the holes in the ends of the metal ties; whereupon the bolts are given a part turn so that the projections will hold the tie in place, the nuts are screwed up tight and the two sides of the wooden form and the central insulating boards are thus held rigidly in position the required distance apart.

A sufficient number of wooden forms are constructed to allow them to be placed around the foundation of the house, in two rows, one above the other, and the upper row is fitted to the one below by means of the cleats as shown in Figures 1 and 3, with the central insulating boards and reinforcing ties in place as just described. The mixture of concrete is then poured in from above until it fills the spaces between the sides of the wooden forms and the central boards, and as the mixture is sufficiently liquid to spread and fill all the crevices, a solid wall is obtained.

This is left standing until it has set, after which the lower of the series of wooden forms is removed by simply loosening the nuts that hold the securing bolts, giving each bolt a slight turn to allow its head and projections to be withdrawn through the hole and notches in the bent end of the metal tie, and then pulling away bolts, inside washer and wooden forms from both sides of the concrete wall. This leaves a solid construction consisting of two thicknesses of concrete with the continuous insulating boards in the center, all held together rigidly by the metal reinforcing ties which are left embedded in the wall.

The holes left in the sides of the concrete by the removal of the inside washers are pointed

ECONOMICAL CONCRETE CONSTRUCTION

up with a trowel, and any ridges or unevenness caused by the joint or roughness of the boards are smoothed off with a wooden float. This gives an interesting sand finish to the concrete, and if a perfectly smooth finish is desired a steel trowel may be used and a skim coat applied.

Another series of central insulating boards, C, is then fitted above those of the second row, provided with metal reinforcing ties, A, with the bottom row of forms, just removed, fastened on either side of the central insulating boards, the cleats being always arranged in staggered relation as shown in the drawings. The bolts are then tightened and concrete is again poured into the molds around the walls of the house.

This process is repeated, one layer of concrete being cast each day, until the entire outer walls are completed. By estimating the amount of time and labor required for each daily operation, the exact number of men needed can be employed, putting the work on a most economical basis.

One of the most practical features of this construction is the simple way in which the doors and windows are set into the outside

FIG. 3: VIEW OF PART OF TWO WOODEN FORMS DURING CASTING OPERATION, SHOWING ARRANGEMENT OF CLEATS, METAL TIES, INSULATING BOARDS AND CONCRETE.

walls. In building up the forms and casting the successive layers of concrete around the house, wherever such an opening is needed, the rough frame of a door or window is placed inside the wooden forms, with the sides of the frame at right angles to the sides of the forms: see Figure 1. This frame, which consists of side and top boards, rests on the hardened concrete layer below, and is temporarily fastened to the forms to hold it in place while the wall is being cast. It is provided with vertical grooves, as shown in Figure 4, to insure its being locked firmly in the concrete. As this rough frame is only 4 inches wide and the wall is 8 inches wide, a temporary rough inner frame, 8 inches wide, is fastened to the 4-inch frame, thus closing the door or window opening during the casting operation. The concrete is then poured into

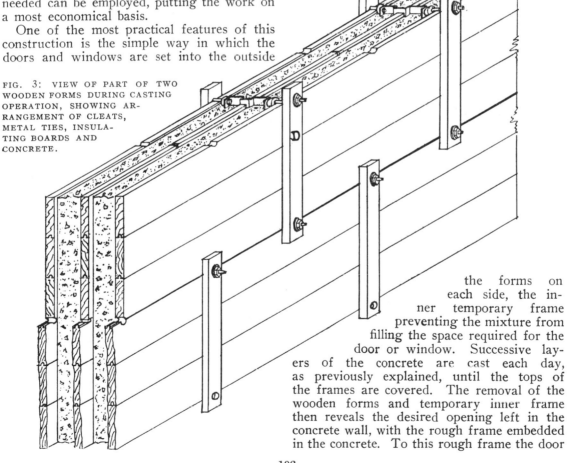

the forms on each side, the inner temporary frame preventing the mixture from filling the space required for the door or window. Successive layers of the concrete are cast each day, as previously explained, until the tops of the frames are covered. The removal of the wooden forms and temporary inner frame then reveals the desired opening left in the concrete wall, with the rough frame embedded in the concrete. To this rough frame the door

193

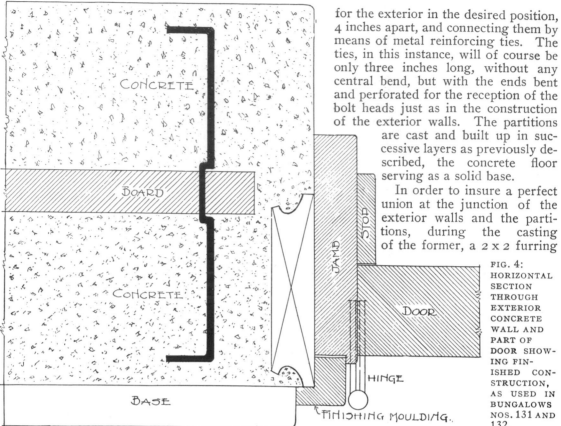

for the exterior in the desired position, 4 inches apart, and connecting them by means of metal reinforcing ties. The ties, in this instance, will of course be only three inches long, without any central bend, but with the ends bent and perforated for the reception of the bolt heads just as in the construction of the exterior walls. The partitions are cast and built up in successive layers as previously described, the concrete floor serving as a solid base.

In order to insure a perfect union at the junction of the exterior walls and the partitions, during the casting of the former, a 2 x 2 furring

FIG. 4: HORIZONTAL SECTION THROUGH EXTERIOR CONCRETE WALL AND PART OF DOOR SHOWING FINISHED CONSTRUCTION, AS USED IN BUNGALOWS NOS. 131 AND 132.

or window jambs may afterward be fastened, leaving a concrete reveal. When several windows are grouped together, making an extra wide opening in the wall, like those shown in Figure 1, the top of the opening is reinforced to center the load, and the frame is propped in the middle until the mullions are inserted, after which the prop may be removed.

From this description and the drawings it will be seen that the walls are cast in successive layers all around the house, unhindered by the door and window openings, which are thus provided for at the same time.

The interior or partition walls of the bungalow are somewhat different in construction, for the temperature on either side of them will be practically the same, no moisture will condense, and so no central insulation will be needed. For these partitions, therefore, solid concrete can be used. Each partition is 4 inches thick and is made by placing the wooden forms used

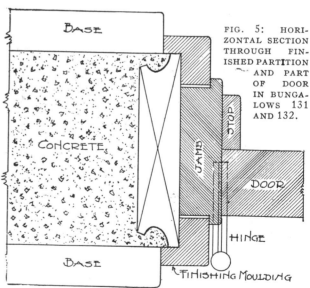

FIG. 5: HORIZONTAL SECTION THROUGH FINISHED PARTITION AND PART OF DOOR IN BUNGALOWS 131 AND 132.

ECONOMICAL CONCRETE CONSTRUCTION

strip is placed upright on the inner side, within the wooden form, at the point from which the partition wall is to extend. When the forms are removed this furring strip is also pulled away, leaving a vertical groove on the inner side of the concrete wall. Afterward, when the partition is being cast, the concrete poured into the wooden forms fills this vertical groove, hardens, and ties the outside and inside walls of the house firmly together. Thus when the whole has been cast, foundation, walls and partitions will form practically an integral construction.

Usually, in building a house, the interior trimming is one of the most expensive items, often representing one-fourth of the total building cost, for it involves both expensive materials and skilled carpentering. With the method of construction used here, however, this expense is reduced to a minimum.

In constructing the partitions of these bungalows, openings are left in the 4-inch concrete walls by inserting rough wooden frames within the wooden forms and casting the wall around them just as in the case of the exterior walls, the rough wooden frames serving as a foundation to which the door jambs are afterward fastened. In this instance, however, no temporary inner frame is needed, the walls and rough frames being the same width. This construction will be seen clearly by reference to Figure 5, which shows, in horizontal section, the concrete partition with baseboards on either side, the rough frame embedded in the concrete, the door jamb fastened to the rough frame and rabbeted to receive the finishing moldings, the rabbet being sufficiently deep to prevent any crack showing if the wood shrinks, and tight enough to insure a close fit between jamb and moldings. The

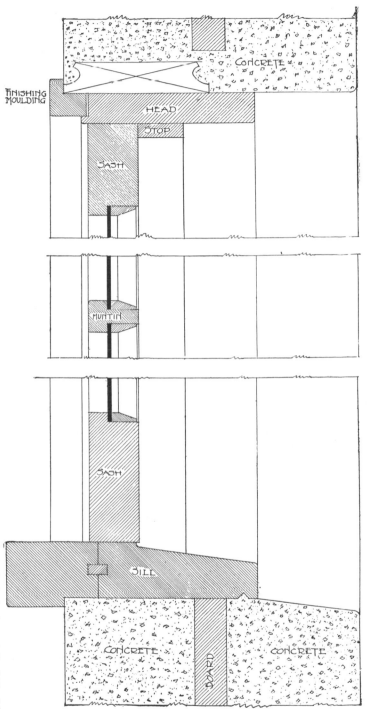

FIG. 6: VERTICAL SECTION THROUGH WINDOW IN CONCRETE CONSTRUCTION USED FOR BUNGALOWS NOS. 131 AND 132, SHOWING HOW THE VARIOUS PARTS ARE SET INTO THE OPENING IN THE CONCRETE WALL.

195

Published in The Craftsman, March, 1912.

ONE-STORY CONCRETE BUNGALOW SHOWING PRACTICAL AND DECORATIVE USE OF WOODEN BEAMS FOR PILLARS AND GABLE OF PORCH: THE ECONOMICAL FORM OF CONCRETE CONSTRUCTION USED HERE IS EXPLAINED IN DESCRIPTION AND WORKING DRAWINGS: NO. 132.

door stop is fastened to the jamb and the door is hung in the usual way. The edges of the rough frame will serve as "grounds" for the plasterer.

These parts and similar parts for the windows, constitute practically all the interior trimmings required, and the material can be got out in the mill and sent to the job already stained and finished, so that all which is needed is for the carpenter to miter the pieces at the corners and put them in place. In this way the whole interior can be trimmed at little labor and expense, compared with that usually incurred.

The gables of both bungalows are shingled, the roofs are of Ruberoid, and the chimneys, though shown of concrete, would be equally or possibly more satisfactory if of brick. In each case the rooms are all on one floor, as compact as possible and yet with a hospitable sense of openness in the arrangement of living and dining rooms, inglenook and porch spaces.

In bungalow No. 131 the entrance door leads from the recessed corner porch, with its concrete pillars, parapets and flower-boxes, directly into the spacious living room, made cheerful by three pleasant window groups and by the welcome vista of the inglenook at the farther end. From the dining room, through another wide opening, a glimpse is also had of this pleasant nook, with its open hearth, built-in bookshelves and fireside seats, so that both rooms share its comfort and friendliness. An interesting feature of the left-hand fireside seat is the fact that it may serve as a storage place for coal, which may be put in from the kitchen and taken out in the nook as needed for the fire.

From the dining room a door leads to the corner porch at the rear, where meals can be served in warm weather. Doors also lead from the dining room and porch to a small square passageway communicating with the kitchen and pantry. The kitchen in turn opens upon a recessed porch which will serve as an outside kitchen or laundry. Off one side of this porch is the coal bin and a door to the maid's room, which is provided with a lavatory. Two bedrooms, bathroom and ample closets occupy the rest of the floor plan, being shut off from the living room by a small hallway.

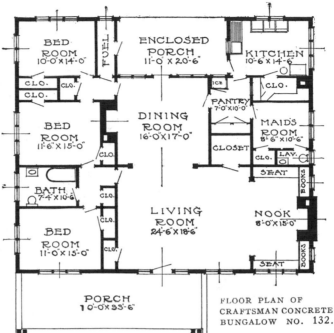

FLOOR PLAN OF CRAFTSMAN CONCRETE BUNGALOW NO. 132.

In bungalow No. 132 a somewhat different arrangement is shown. The large living room and dining room are planned with only a slight division between, so that upon entering from the front porch one has a vista through both rooms to the dining-room windows in the rear which overlook the enclosed porch. The inglenook occupies the whole right-hand end of the living room, and on each side of the chimneypiece are built-in bookcases and seats. A large closet is also provided, and a smaller closet is placed at the left of the entrance door for umbrellas, wraps, etc. A fireplace is also built in the dining room. In one corner of the plan are pantry, kitchen, maid's room and lavatory, with ample closet space and shelves. The kitchen communicates with the enclosed porch at the rear, which will serve as an open-air dining and living room, and on the opposite side of which is a place for fuel. Three bedrooms and bathroom are provided on this side of the bungalow, with plenty of closets both in the rooms and in the small hallways between them.

The compactness of both bungalows will minimize the household work, and either design would be suitable for those who do not wish to keep a maid, as the bedroom set aside for that purpose would serve equally well for one of the family.

THE CRAFTSMAN FIREPLACE: A COMPLETE HEATING AND VENTILATING SYSTEM

O N account of the number of inquiries that have been received in regard to the Craftsman fireplace-furnace, I have thought it advisable to publish another description and set of drawings, embodying several improvements over the form of fireplace originally shown. These improvements have simplified not only the construction of the heater but also the work of installing it.

As shown in Figures 1, 2 and 3, the heater body is made of large sheets of steel, welded together by special welding machinery into

VIEW OF CRAFTSMAN FIREPLACE OF TAPESTRY BRICK, WITH OPEN HEARTH AND ANDIRONS FOR BURNING WOOD.

one piece of continuous metal, making leakage of gas, smoke or dust an impossibility. It is so constructed that each smoke compartment is self-cleaning; the smoke areas being vertical, there is no place for soot and moisture to collect. The heater is six feet high and four feet wide and weighs complete with grates and other iron parts needed in the construction about 1,000 pounds.

Grates for the burning of coal or coke are supplied with each heater. These consist of only three parts and are easily and quickly set in place. Figure 1 shows the removable metal hearth and grates in place for the burning of coal. The ashes sift through the grate into the ash pit, which is so large that it needs emptying only once a season. This also eliminates the objectionable feature of dust from the ashes escaping into the room. If it is desired to burn wood upon an open hearth, the metal hearth and grates are removed and the opening into the ash pit is covered by a metal plate on which andirons may be placed for burning wood, as shown in the photograph. Whether the fireplace is equipped with hearth and grates for the burning of coal, or is arranged with open hearth and andirons for the burning of wood, the impression given is at once satisfactory and permanent.

The heater is set on the floor level, and the installation consists in merely building a four-inch brick wall around it. This wall, carried up to the ceiling and roofed over, forms the warm air chamber above the furnace body. In one leg of the chimneypiece is set a smoke flue, shown by dotted lines in Figure 2, which is connected with the body of the heater. I furnish one section of this flue lining, having three holes: one which fits onto the flange around the smoke outlet of the heater, another which may be connected with a pipe from the kitchen range, and a third which opens by register into the room for the purpose of checking the coal fire, but which is

FIGURE 1.

VERTICAL SECTION THROUGH CENTER OF CRAFTSMAN FIREPLACE.

kept closed when wood is burned. This flue starts at the bottom of the smoke outlet on the heater, shown in Figure 3, leaving the leg

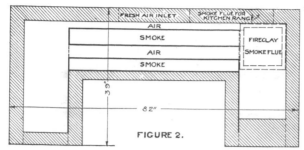

FIGURE 2.

SECTIONAL PLAN OF THE CRAFTSMAN FIREPLACE.

of the chimney below the flue free for the circulation of air.

Any mason can build the wall and make a correct installation. The cost of the brickwork complete with chimney is less than for the usual fireplace of equal size. About 3,000 brick are required where there is a cellar and the chimney is carried up two stories. At a cost of $10.00 per thousand for brick and an equal sum per thousand for sand, cement and labor, the entire cost of brickwork, including $5.00 for flue lining, would be about $65.00.

I have used the common hard-burned brick as a basis for the above figures; where the owner desires to make the fireplace of plaster, stone, Tapestry brick or tile, the additional cost will depend upon the material selected. Hard-burned brick laid up with a wide mortar joint will make a beautiful fireplace. There are no limitations as to the design of the chimneypiece, the only requirement being that the inside measurements are kept to those shown in Figure 2.

The Craftsman fireplace may be installed in houses already built, as well as in new ones, the work in each case requiring a new chimney and the cost being practically the same. Because of the universal favor of the open fire it seems best to make only a medium-sized heater, as many people would prefer to have two or even more fireplaces in different parts of the house. The piping of warm air to the various rooms is then a small factor of the cost, as the pipes will be few and short. These are to be furnished by the owner, since they are always in stock at the local hardware store and are inexpensive.

The operation of the heater itself is as follows: As shown in Figure 1 the smoke generated by the fire passes up through the smoke compartment, down behind the steel smoke wall to the bottom of the heater, then up through another smoke compartment to the

smoke outlet flue shown in Figure 3, and out through the chimney.

During its passage the smoke heats the steel walls of the smoke compartments, which in turn heat the air in the air compartments, as will be seen by reference to Figures 1 and 2. The air is thus caused to rise and pass up into the warm air chamber. This action draws in outside air through the fresh air inlet, up through the air compartments into the warm air chamber. At the same time air is also being drawn in from the room through the registers at the base of the fireplace, up through the air compartments into the warm air chamber, where it mixes with the warmed fresh air from outside. The warmed air passes through the upper registers into rooms on the first floor and also through the air pipes to the upper rooms. These air pipes and registers are proportioned in size so that each one will deliver the proper amount of air to the various rooms.

The warm air, upon entering each of the upper rooms, being lightest, rises and spreads out in an even layer against the ceiling. This layer, as it cools, descends to the floor and passes out under the door, down the stairway opening to the lower floor. Part of this air is drawn into the fire and passes out through the chimney, and the rest is drawn into the lower registers. The circulation is rapid and positive, being accomplished, as seen, by gravitation, the heavier or colder air seeking the lowest level and the lighter or warmer air the highest. The heater thus maintains a constant circulation between the various rooms as well as a movement of the air within the rooms, making a given air supply go much farther than with other heating systems.

In this circulation, the air absorbs all impurities, and naturally the zone of the most vitiated air is nearest the floor. It is from this zone that the fireplace draws immense quantities of air and discharges it through the chimney. An adult vitiates from 2,500 to 3,000 cubic feet of air per hour. The fireplace is constructed to admit 20,-000 cubic feet of fresh air and discharge through the chimney the same amount of vitiated or used air per hour, thus making perfect ventilation for seven adults. In this way the air throughout the house is entirely replaced with fresh warmed air from outdoors every fifteen or twenty minutes. Doors and windows should be kept closed in order that the circulation of air may not be disturbed, for upon the proper circulation depends the efficient heating and ventilating of the house. Under these conditions there can be no drafts.

The danger of the fireplace smoking is entirely eliminated, as the smoke and air openings are properly proportioned and, being part of the steel body, do not depend upon the judgment of the mason. Moreover, it is not only impossible for back drafts to force smoke into the room, but sparks are prevented from escaping through the flue, thereby removing all danger of fire on the roof.

The conserving within the brick walls of all heat which has formerly been lost in the cellar; the circulating of volumes of air in contact with the large areas of smoke surface, thereby extracting practically all the heat from the smoke, and the radiation of heat direct into the room from the open fire, make the Craftsman fireplace a most efficient heating system. One fireplace will amply heat a seven-room house, with a consumption of from seven to ten tons of coal per year in a climate like that of our Central States. The exact amount of fuel consumed, however, depends largely upon the exposure, the number and size of the windows, and the construction of the house. Coal or coke will furnish a more even and steady heat both day and night than wood, but because of the slow combustion due to the down draft, wood may be used as a fuel with entire satisfaction from a standpoint of both economy and attention. Then, too, the wood fire is so much quicker than coal or coke in producing heat and so easily started that its use will be almost universal for fuel during the late fall and early spring.

The price of the steel heater complete with grates, registers and all metal parts (except the pipes needed to conduct warm air from the heater to rooms distant from it) amounts, with the freight, to $150.00. By combining this with the cost of the brickwork and the pipes one can easily install the heating plant complete inside of $250.00. The fireplace is sold only direct to users. I require the plans of each house in which it is to be installed, and from them I make and furnish free to the owner a heating layout which shows the location and size of warm air pipes and registers, and includes complete plans and instruc-

tions for the mason to use in building the brickwork. I guarantee the fireplace to heat and ventilate properly each house in which it is installed, and by making the heating plant myself and selling it direct to users, I am in a position to assume the entire responsibility of its giving satisfaction.

I am ready to make shipments of Craftsman fireplaces, and shall be glad to hear from all those who are considering the installation of

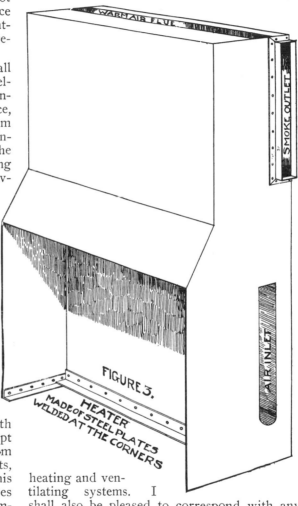

FIGURE 3.

heating and ventilating systems. I shall also be pleased to correspond with any readers who may wish further explanation of the construction of the heater and the manner of its operation.